カムカムエヴリバディ

Family English

福田昇八／平川洌 編
トム・リード 校閲

20×10

南雲堂

音声ファイル
無料 DL
のご案内

この書籍の音声を無料で視聴（ストリーミング）・ダウンロードできます。自習用音声としてご活用ください。（添付の CD と同じコンテンツです。）
以下のサイトにアクセスして書籍番号で検索してください。

https://nanun-do.com　テキスト番号［ **087394** ］

※ 無線 LAN（WiFi）に接続してのご利用を推奨いたします。

※ 音声ダウンロードは Zip ファイルでの提供になります。
お使いの機器によっては別途ソフトウェア（アプリケーション）の導入が必要となります。

ファミリーイングリッシュ音声ダウンロードページは
左記の QR コードからもご利用になれます。

まえがき

21 世紀にも通用する英語

本書は、昭和 21 年から 5 年間にわたり NHK で放送された平川唯一講師担当の英語会話講座のラジオテキスト全 54 冊 216 話から 20 話を選んで編集したものである。平川英語には幼稚園児や小学低学年を主人公とする話が多いが、本書では、年齢が上の人物の話を多く採用した。

原著の本文は戦前の英語で書かれている。これを現在のアメリカ日常英語になるよう、ワシントン・ポスト紙記者トム・リード氏に修正してもらった。

注釈は、原著の「活用」に基づき編者が加筆修正を加えたものである。ここには理解を深め、英語運用力をつけるような例文を多くつけ加え、最後に実力を知るための「英語で言ってみよう」をつけた。語学は要するにドリルである。決まり文句を繰り返し言ってみて覚えてしまうほかはない。原著には英語の文章の読みがカタカナで示されていた。これは単語の発音でなく英文の文章全体の発音を示すという点で画期的な工夫であった。本書では、このカナ表記を割愛し、代りに付属音声の利用ができるようにした。

家族英語はことばの基礎

平川英語は言葉の基礎をなす家族の会話を題材としている。日本人が暮らしのなかで使っている言葉を英語でどう言うか、これを教えるのが家族英語である。平川英語は、「人間は母国語を親から口まねによって学ぶのであるから、英語を学ぶのも、これと同じく口まね方式が最高である」という考えに基づく。

母国語は、まず親の言うことを聞き取り、それを口まねすることによって習得する。英語も口まねなら誰にでもできる。文字と文法は後回しにして、まず文章全体を覚えよう。こうすることで誰でも会話が習得できる。

家族の会話はあまり高級なものではない。それで子供っぽく感じられて当然である。しかしながら、例えば、「どこに行ってたの」とか、「ぼくも行きたいなあ」などが言えなくては、英語の基礎を身につけることはできない。日本語とは違って、英語では、子供の言葉はそのまま大人の言葉であることを知っておきたい。

文法的には高級な家族のことば

家族英語は文法的には高級である。最初から、過去形も未来形も完了形も仮定法も出てくる。文法的に見れば、これは大学受験程度と言ってよい。慣用的な表現も、文法的に説明すれば難しい。こんなのがすべて家族英語に入っている。これを口まねで言うのは簡単で、口まねなら小学生でも簡単にできる。文字でどう書くかは考えなくてよい。ただ付属音声の会話を繰り返し聞いて、まねをすればよい。耳に聞こえたとおりに口で言うだけでよい。

本書の家族英語は終戦直後の貧しい生活のなかから生まれた。当時の生活を偲ぶ意味もあって、本文はあえて元のままの内容で残した。貧しい生活の中に豊かな心があったことを若い読者に感じていただければ幸いである。確かに、停電を知らない世代の人には、「停電になったらどうしよう」などという会話は、時代錯誤も甚だしいと言わねばならない。しかし、われわれは時代に迎合（げいごう）するには及（およ）ばない。古いことも新しいことも、それを表現する基本構文は不変である。

まず英語の先生たちが家族英語を

私はまず、中学高校で英語を教えている人たちに家族英語をすすめたい。生徒たちは日常のことを英語で言ってみたいという強い欲望（よくぼう）をもっている。この本には、役に立つ言い方がたくさんあるのだから、授業の始めに毎日一つの言い方を教えるだけで良い。それが生徒を喜ばせ、落ちこぼれのいない英語クラスを実現できるのではないか。私はそのような願いを込めてこの本を作った。これからの重要テーマとなる小学英語にも、この本は役に立つはずである。

中学生や高校生が本書を使うときは、一つの話を完全にものにするまで次の話には進まないほうがよい。一つの話に２週間かかっても１か月かかってもよい。学校英語だけでは、決して身につくことのない会話力が身につく。それが家族英語である。

編者

福田昇八

Foreword

Nearly three quarters of a century has passed since my father known throughout this land as "Come Come English Ojisan" graced the radio waves with his vibrant voice. Supposedly just a 15-minutes English conversation class, the program eradicated the fear of learning foreign language and brought smiles, hope, and belief in better tomorrows into war-ravaged family rooms.

Tadaichi Hirakawa was a perfectionist. Thus, not a single word was spoken into the microphone during the 15-minute broadcast that he had not carefully chosen for the six pages of manuscript that he read every broadcast. His love and commitment to his listeners was reflected in the texts which contained all the delightful stories that unfolded during a week of broadcasts.

It was no accident that the most of the stories in the texts were "family scenes". Dad believed the rebuilding of Japan must start with the foundation of strong family unity and with the ability to communicate with the world. In his later years, it gave my father immeasurable pleasure to hear prominent bankers and presidents of highly visible multi-national manufacturing and trading companies say: "My start in an international career was made possible because I listened every evening to the Come Come English program."

The Hirakawa family is most grateful for the tremendous efforts of Professor Shohachi Fukuda (himself a "Come Come Baby"!) who spared no efforts to accomplish a renaissance of Hirakawa's so lovingly crafted text. We also appreciate Mr. T. R. Reid's significant contribution of updating some of the expressions to reflect current English usage. Of course, the renaissance would not have been possible were it not for the dedication with which Mr. Atsushi Kato, the editor, pursued this major project. We also wish to thank Ms. Carol Frankel, Emeritus Dean of the school of Education at the University of Puget Sound, Ms. Ariel Watanabe & her father Mr. Eric Dennison and Mr. John Utz for the help of proof-reading of this book.

Professor Fukuda promised my deceased mother that he would bring this project to fruition. I am sure "Mama" is sitting with Dad nodding vigorously as a gesture of acknowledgement. For them, an added pleasure is to know that granddaughter Hanako Kagaya provided all the illustrations for this book.

The EDO-TOKYO MUSEUM proudly displays originals of

Hirakawa's texts. These are in mint condition and the museum affords them great care. The curator explained to me that they made an exception to their general policy by choosing to display a specific individual's historical contribution. He said "After all, Mr. Hirakawa is an important part of the postwar history".

It is a singular pleasure for the Hirakawa family that the drama entitled "Come Come Everybody" will be broadcast from November 2021~March 2022 by NHK TV domestically and also broadcast internationally. We are profoundly grateful for their dedication to this project.

Tadaichi Hirakawa's message to his fellow Japanese citizens remains as valid and valuable in the twenty-first century as it was when the live broadcast was first being heard. Let this book be the gateway to a better and happier Japan and the world.

October, 2021
Kiyoshi Hirakawa,
Second Son of Tadaichi Hirakawa

歴史の流れの中で果たされたもの

石原 慎太郎

二十年ほど前に入った、仕事場から間近い南麻布の東京ローンテニスクラブに仕事の合間を見ていく度、いつも小柄で白髪の頭を短く刈った、当時から流行りだしていたフレイムの大きなラケットを胸に抱きしめるような妙なフォームから振り回し、小柄のせいかぴょんぴょん飛び跳ねるような仕種で、しかしなかなかしたたかなテニスをする老人がいた。みんなが先生々々と呼んでいるので多分どこかのお医者さんだろうと思っていたら、暫くしてから、その老人こそ誰あろうかつてラジオを通じて英語教育で一世を風靡した、かのカムカム小父さんと知った。そう知らされて眺める、というより、当時はテレビなどありはしなかったのだから、耳を澄ませて聞き直すと、お年からして当然以前よりは少し声の艶は落ちてはいたが、まちがいなくあの懐かしいカムカム小父さんの声だった。そしてそう悟って改めて、あれからこの国この社会に過ぎていった時間をしみじみ感じさせられたものだった。

私もまたあの頃のカムカム英語の生徒の一人だったが、毎月発行される簡単粗末なテキストを手にして眺めた時の印象を忘れられない。そして平川先生のレッスンは、時節柄あちこちで大流行りだった英語レッスンの中でも際だってユニークかつ楽しいものだった。なにしろ日本生まれの白系ロシア人のジャイアンツのスタルヒン投手が、顔形はとにかく純粋な白人だというだけで彼にとっては母国語であるはずのない英語のレッスンを受け持つような時代だったから。

私自身はあまり熱心な生徒とはいえず、ラジオで学ぶより、はるかに楽しいアメリカ映画を頻繁に見て、画面に出るスーパーインポーズと役者の生の会話を聞き比べメモをとりながら趣味と実益をそなえた勉強法（？）に変えてしまったが、それにしてもその後高校から大学を通じて受けた語学教育の下らなさ、つまらなさにはうんざりし通しだった。

テニスを通じてかつてのカムカム小父さんに会遇してみて、そんな思い出を思いくらべながら、改めて平川先生のかつてのレッスンの秀でた独自性に感心させられたものだ。

テニスにおいてもカムカム小父さんはなかなか良き師で、ある時私のプレイがなぜか思いがけなく不調で出来が悪く腐っていたから、

「そういう時は、自分でも気づかぬことで必ずどこか疲れているものです。だからラケットのグリップをほんの半握り短く持ってみるだけで、ずっと楽に軽く感じられますよ」

などとまことに理にかなったアドバイスをされたりしたものだった。

当時日本は有史以来初めて、外国との戦争で領土まで犯されて破れた衝撃のもたらす有形無形の混乱の中にあった。日本を占領している米軍の最高司令官マッカーサーが過去の日本の文化的成熟もよく知らずに、日本人は年齢でいえば十二歳程度などと滑稽僭越にも断じてみせれば、我々はただただ頭を垂れてそれを聞くしかなかった。いずれにせよ我々は好むと好まざるとに関わらずアメリカという異文化の影響に晒され、下手をすれば精神的な植民地をも受けかねぬ時代にあった。

私自身は戦争に間一髪遅れてきた少年だったが、それでも警

戒警報下急いで下校する途中いきなり艦載機に襲われ、身を投げて隠れた麦畑の背高い穂の間から怖々覗いて仰いだ空を飛び去る敵国戦闘機の胴体に描かれた、毒々しくも鮮やかな漫画を命がけで眺めて感じた異文化への戦慄（せんりつ）を忘れられない。そして終戦後わずか数日に、私の住んでいた逗子沖の相模湾に集結したアメリカの大艦隊のすさまじいほどの偉容を必死に受け止めたことも忘れられない。

そんな意識の状況下で、我々は質的にも量的にも全く異なるアメリカ文化を、戦後ほぼ一方的に受け入れさせられてきた。そして英語はその摂取のための絶対必要条件でもあった。人々は周章狼狽（しゅうしょうろうばい）しながらもむさぼるように、タブーとまでされていたかつての敵国語の修得に争い努めたものだ。

しかしそうした戦後の国家的ともいえる作業を手助けした教師の一人として、他の誰よりも明るく、日本人には珍しくウィットに富み、そしてこの伝記を読んで初めて知らされる、アメリカでの長き滞在の中の苦労に培（つちか）われた日本人としての気骨をも供えたカムカム小父さんを持ったということは、社会全体にとっていかに僥倖（ぎょうこう）であったことか。

人間は歴史の流れの中で、時として自分自身も意識せぬある貴重な役割を果たすものなのだということを、カムカム小父さんは教えてくれる。

（いしはらしんたろう・作家）

『カムカム　エブリバディ　平川唯一と「カムカム英語」の時代』NHK出版より転載

めぐりあい

田崎 清忠

飛行機の設計をやりたいと願って府立航空工業学校に入学したのに、2年生のとき戦争が終わり、日本では飛行機を作ることが禁止されてしまいました。「夢」を奪(うば)われた少年はただ無為(むい)に毎日を過ごすばかり。そこに現れたのが「カムカム英語」でした。ラジオから聞こえてくるカムカムおじさんから英語だけではなく「元気」をもらい、あっという間に番組のとりこになりました。人は一生の間に、人生を形作る何らかの「めぐりあい」を体験するものです。思えば、平川先生は私にとって貴重な最初のめぐりあいでした。

工業学校にいながら、機械設計や工作機械などの科目よりも英語に熱中し、卒業するころには地元の中学校から「代用英語教員(だいようえいごきょういん)」にならないかとの誘(さそ)いを受けました。貧(まず)しかった我が家で、高等教育を受ける費用をひねり出すことは困難(こんなん)。代用教員の道を選ぼうと決心しました。そのとき、「第二のめぐりあい」が訪(おとず)れました。近所の獣医さんが教えてくれたのです。「高等師範(こうとうしはん)学校に行けばいい。学費ゼロで毎月給費も出るよ」。

あとは英語の道をまっしぐら。フルブライト留学制度でアメリカへ。帰国してしばらくするとNHKテレビ英語会話の講師に。当時英語教育分野で最先端の構造主義言語学と視聴覚教育を放送に取り入れるための努力が続きました。そんなときにも、忘れられないのは平川先生からいただいたご恩(おん)。そしてあるとき、番組のゲストとしてお迎えすることにしました。スタジオの重いドアが開いて先生のお姿がライトの下に現れたとき、私は感動で胸が詰まり、とめどなく涙が流れました。「こんにちは、たざきさん」･･･少年時代に毎日耳にしていた時そのままの優しいお声。戦後一世を風靡（ふうび）した「カムカム英語」の先生が目の前におられるのです。私は「カムカムベィビィ」に戻っていました。

2020年に私は90歳になりました。今はパソコンを利用して、さまざまな情報を発信しています。私との「めぐりあい」がひとりでも多くの人の役に立つことを願って。

（たざき・きよただ / 横浜国立大学名誉教授、元NHKテレビ英語会話講師）

平川唯一ギャラリー
高梁市歴史美術館蔵

放送中の平川唯一

出版記念パーティー

学生をスタジオに招いて

平川唯一『カムカム英語（英語会話）』の特色

1. 苦い顔の努力や勉強はやめて、英語をやたらにもてあそぶこと。

2. 赤ちゃんになったつもりで、講師の発音や言葉の調子をまねること。

3. なるべく一家そろって、英会話の時間をつくること。

4. 恥ずかしがる気持ちを完全に捨てて、習った言葉を家庭で実際に使うこと。

5. 片言でも日本語交じりでもよいから、考え込まず、英語の形で会話を運ぶこと。

Contents

コラム

音楽
ハワイの結婚の歌～「ブルー・ハワイ」
（『ウクレレ・パラダイスII　懐かしの映画音楽』）
Track 1, 3, 5, 9, 12

ヒロ・マーチ
（『UKULELE MAGIC ～踊るウクレレ』）演奏：平川 洌
Track 1, 6, 10, 13, 15, 18,

第三の男
（『ウクレレ・パラダイスII　懐かしの映画音楽』）
演奏：平川 洌とハッピー・スターズ／ウクレレ・ソロ：平川 洌
Track 2, 7, 11, 14, 17

アロハ・オエ
（『UKULELE MAGIC ～踊るウクレレ』）演奏：平川 洌
Track 4, 8, 16, 20

『ウクレレ・パラダイスII　懐かしの映画音楽』
演奏：平川 洌とハッピー・スターズ／ウクレレ・ソロ：平川 洌
発売諸：（株）ジェーピー・インターナショナル　JPI-7064
『UKULELE MAGIC ～踊るウクレレ』
演奏：平川 洌
発売諸：（株）ジェーピー・インターナショナル　JPI-7082

本文イラスト：ものづくり 波奈子

Dialog One

ALL EVEN
勝負なし

これは時代を超えた親子の会話である。弁当を入れ忘れたお母さん、それに気付かずに出かけたお父さん、こんな日常を題材にして最後は格言めいた言葉で締める筆者の腕は何度読んでも飽きない。これが平川英語の品の良さであろう。

その後、聞いたところでは、平川講師は夕方 6 時からの放送のために、朝早くから NHK へ行き、15 分間放送するための原稿を書いて繰り返しリハーサルをしたという。あの充実した講師の語り口の見事さには、それだけの準備があったのである。本書は当時のテキストを少し味付けしただけで、放送時のあの温かい語り掛けの片鱗も伝えることはできない。わずかに「赤ちゃんの口まねのように、楽しく、にこにこと口まねをしておれば皆さんも必ず自然と上手になることができるのですよ」という言葉が口癖であったことだけをここに伝えることができる。

ALL EVEN

Track-02

Taro: Dad, wait for me!

Dad: What's the big rush? You have plenty of time before school.

Taro: Boy, I'm out of breath. You're a fast walker, Dad.

Dad: I'm in a hurry this morning, that's why.

Taro: I thought I could catch up with you at the corner.

Dad: Did you run all the way from the house?

Taro: Yes, as fast as I could.

Dad: No wonder you're sweating.

Taro: Funny, you never forget your umbrella.

Dad: Never. Didn't you bring yours? It's going to rain today.

Taro: Mine's at school.

Dad: You mean, you forgot it there?

Taro: Well, when you take an umbrella, it usually doesn't rain.

Dad: You never can tell.

Taro: But, Dad, you forgot something more important.

Dad: I have my briefcase here. My wallet and pass are in my pocket.

Taro: What about this?

Dad: Oh, my lunch. I thought my briefcase was too light.

Taro: Mom had forgotten to put it in there.

Dad: That makes us even. We all forget now and then, don't we?

太郎　お父さん、待って。

父　なんでそうあわてる。まだ学校は早いだろう。

太郎　あーあ、息がきれちゃった。お父さんは歩くのが速いんだね。

父　今朝はちょっと急いでいるからだよ。

太郎　ぼく、あの角(かど)のあたりで追いつけると思ったんだけど。

父　家からずっと走って来たのかい。

太郎　そう、一生懸命(いっしょうけんめい)で。

父　だから汗をかいているんだな。

太郎　お父さんは不思議と傘(かさ)だけは忘れないね。

父　忘れないさ。太郎はどうした。今日は降るよ。

太郎　ぼくのは学校に置いてある。

父　なんだ、忘れたのか。

太郎　だって傘を持って行くと、たいてい降らないんだから。

父　しかし分からないよ。

太郎　でもお父さんはもっと大事なものを忘れているよ。

父　鞄(かばん)は持っているし、財布もパスもポケットに入ってる。

太郎　これはどう。

父　あっ、弁当か。どうも鞄が軽いと思ったよ。

太郎　お母さんが鞄に入れるのを忘れたんだって。

父　じゃ、みんな同じだ。誰でも時には忘れるものだね。

Point 1

Taro: **Dad, wait for me!**
Dad: **What's the big rush? You have plenty of time before school.**
Taro: **Boy, I'm out of breath. You're a fast walker, Dad.**
Dad: **I'm in a hurry this morning, that's why.**
Taro: **I thought I could catch up with you at the corner.**

Wait for me.「待って。」この for me にあたる言葉は日本語では使わないが、英語では必要であるから注意。

What's the big rush?「何をあわてているのか。」あわてるというのを英語で何と言うか、などと考えて苦労するより、こうした会話用語を身につけたほうが、ずっと実用的である。

have plenty of time「時間は十分ある」

out of breath「息切れがする」何でも足りなくなって、無くなるのを out of ... という。

I'm out of paper.「紙がなくなった。」

We have plenty of money but we are out of time.

a fast walker「歩くのが早い」

I am a good driver.「運転は上手です。」

I am not a good singer.「歌は下手です。」

in a hurry「急いで」hurry の前に in a が付くことは特に注意しないと忘れやすい。

..., that's why. 理由を言うときの決まり文句。

I am hungry, that's why.

I was late, that's why.

catch up with you「あなたに追い付く」これも奇妙な言い方のようであるが、これが極めて普通の言い方なのである。

I'll catch up with you in three months.
「３か月もすれば追いついてみせるよ。」

Point 2

Dad: **Did you run all the way from the house?**
Taro: **Yes, as fast as I could.**
Dad: **No wonder you're sweating.**
Taro: **Funny, you never forget your umbrella.**
Dad: **Never. Didn't you bring yours? It's going to rain today.**

as fast as I could「できるだけ早く as ... as はよく出てくるから実例によって使い方を身につけよう。

Is Jiro as tall as his father?
I always walk as fast as I can.
I always walk as much as I can.
I went as far as I could. 「行ける所まで行った。」

No wonder ...「それで…なのだね」
No wonder you are studying hard.
No wonder you look happy.

Funny, ...「…なのはおかしい」
Funny, you never look tired.
「決して疲れたようには見えないなんておかしい。」
Funny, you never see her.

bring「持ってくる」bringとtakeの使い分けを覚えよう。「持って(連れて)行く」ときはtake ... を、「持って(連れて)来る」ときはbring ... を使う。例文ではcookiesをfriendsにしてもよい。

I took some cookies to the party.
They brought some cookies to the party.

It's going to rain today.「今日は雨が降るよ。」
It's going to clear up today.
It's going to be cloudy all day today.

Point 3

Taro: **Mine's at school.**
Dad: **You mean, you forgot it there?**
Taro: **Well, when you take an umbrella, it usually doesn't rain.**
Dad: **You never can tell.**
Taro: **But, Dad, you forgot something more important.**

Mine's at school.「ぼくのは学校に置いてある。」こんなのも基本になる言い方であるから、応用ができるところまで身につけておきたい。前置詞は語によって変る。

Mine's home. / Mine's in the box.
Yours is at the station. / Yours is in the car.

You mean, ...?「…という意味ですか。」確認するときの言い方。

You mean, you are going to marry her?
You mean, you lost your purse?

You for got it.「おまえは忘れた。」it を落とさないこと。

When you take an umbrella「傘を持って行くと」この主語のyouは「あなた」という意味ではなく、「一般に人は」という意味。次の You never can tell. の主語も同じ。

When you drink, you get sleepy.「飲むと眠くなる。」
When you drive, use your seatbelt.

You never can tell.「分かるもので はない。」tell は「分かる」

You may become a scholar; you never can tell.
「学者になるかもしれない。それはわからない。」
I can't tell the difference.

something more important「もっと大事なもの」

I have something more interesting today.
more useful today.

Point 4

Dad: **I have my briefcase here. My wallet and pass are in my pocket.**
Taro: **What about this?**
Dad: **Oh, my lunch. I thought my briefcase was too light.**
Taro: **Mom had forgotten to put it in there.**
Dad: **That makes us even. We all forget now and then, don't we?**

What about this?「これはどうですか。」this のところを換えれば何にでも使える便利な言い方。例えば What about my car? は、状況により、どこに駐車するか、どうするか、などいろいろな意味になり得る。

I thought ... was too light.「は軽すぎると思った」これは前に「それで」といった感じのことばが略された言い方。英語には日本語のような語尾がなくて、ぶっきらぼうな言い方をするが、それを補うのがイントネーションである。最後の語を上げて下げるような感じで言えば、英語らしくなる。

I thought my bag was too heavy.
I thought he was too kind.
「親切過ぎると思ったよ。」

Mom had forgotten お父さんが弁当を忘れて家を出るより前に、お母さんが鞄に入れるのを忘れていたのだから、過去完了になる。

That makes us even.「それでみんな同じだ。勝負無しだ。」このような that を主語にした言い方も英語の特色。

That made me happy.「それで嬉しくなった。」
That reminds me.「それで思い出したよ。」

now and then = once in a while.「ときどき」

I eat there now and then.

実力チェック　英語で言ってみよう！

1. いま急いでいますので。
2. だから汗かいているのね。
3. 手袋(てぶくろ)を店に忘れて来たって言うのかい。
4. 時には間違いをするものよね。
5. 日本人は世界の大国に追いつくために大(おお)いに働(はたら)いてきた。

父、カムカムおじさんとわたし

Mary 萬里子 大野

昭和21年2月1日にスタートしたカムカムラジオ放送の3ヶ月前に生まれた私「メリー」は、まさにCome Come Babyでした。物心がついてきた3歳頃、父の書斎を覗(のぞ)くとニコニコした笑顔でカムカム放送の原稿を読んでいる姿に「Daddy何が楽しいのかしら？」と不思議に思い、今でもその印象が記憶に焼き付いています。

当時夕方6時になるとラジオから流れる“Come Come Everybody”の歌に小躍(こおど)りしていた私は、日比谷公会堂のカムカム大会で白いドレスを着てカムカムのダンスを踊る楽しさを知り、神田生まれの母に促(うな)され7歳から日本舞踊(ぶよう)のお稽古(けいこ)を始めました。高校生時代の夏休みには米軍基地のワシントンハイツ、グリーンパーク等から子供たちに踊りを教えて欲しいと声が掛かり、父から役に立つ英語のフレーズを習いながら小さな子供たちを相手に絵日傘(えひがさ)やてるてる坊主などを教え始め、自然と英会話もマスターしていきました。それが功を成してか、名取資格取得後30年、現在もSeattle Central College（100年前に父が通ったBroadway Highschool）と自宅スタジオで長唄(ながうた)三味線、日本舞踊を教え、着物の着付け日本語会話のクラス等、Come Come Spiritをもって楽しく教えています。

父はよく「メリーはいろいろなことができるね、でもDaddyは名前の通り、唯一つのことしかできないよ」と褒(ほ)めてくれましたが、とんでもない！　父の手の器用(きよう)なところは誰も真似ができません。愛車、英国のモーリスの修理も自分でおこない、走行メーターが一回転したとか。プロの修理屋さんも「平川先生にはかないません」と。また20畳ほどある居間の壁や天井のペンキ塗りも一人で完璧に仕上げ、ペンキ屋さんも顔負け。母が「Daddy, これ直してちょうだい」と言うと、いつも次の日には『はい』と完全に修理。ものを大切にすることを教えてくれた父。父の完璧な一生を私も真似(まね)したいです。

父の生きたカムカム英語が再び世に拡(ひろ)がり、多くの人が楽しく英語で話すことができる日が来ることを願ってやみません。

（メリー・まりこ おおの／平川唯一 次女）

カムカム英語と私たち

丸山一郎

放送に立ち会って

私たちの日常生活は電子やコンピューター機器でコントロールされているといえましょう。そんな時代に職人気質(きしつ)という言葉は過去のものと考えられるかもしれません。

平川先生の放送・録音に毎回立ち会った一人として今でも強烈(きょうれつ)な印象となっているのはまさにこの放送マン気質です。近ごろのテレビやラジオでは臨場(りんじょう)感を演出するためか、バサバサと原稿をめくる音が耳ざわりですが、カムカム放送で紙の音を聞いた人は一人もいないでしょう。効果音として先生が紙をまるめたことはありますが…。

先生がよどみなくお話になるので大半の聴取(ちょうしゅ)者が「すごい雄弁(ゆうべん)家だ」と考えたことでした。自宅の書斎(しょさい)でストップウォッチを片手に5, 6回放送原稿を読み、スタジオに入ってからも息つぎ、抑揚(よくよう)、ふりがななど原稿に書き込む姿は余人(よじん)の入り込むすきを与えないきびしさがありました。大判の放送原稿の角を少し折り曲げてめくりやすくし、「パペピプペポパポ」と何度もアーティキュレイションの口ならしをなさっていました。「カムカム放送は私の生命」とよくおっしゃっていましたが、私たちカムカムベイビーズが「カムカムスピリット」というファンの気持ちも、こんな先生の意気ごみから学びとった生き方であり、楽しい英語あそびに熱中する事になった要因(よういん)ではないでしょうか。コンピューターに出来ないこともあるようです。

(まるやま・いちろう/カムカムファンクラブ代表・習志野バプテスト教会牧師)
(元・小松川 CCC)

Dialog Two

A GOAT

やぎ

犬や猫はどこにでもいるが、やぎを飼っている家は滅多にない。それは昔もそうだった。この話の良さは、やぎを飼うことを母親に認めてもらうこの子の元気の良さと、やぎの乳とお母さんのおっぱいを結び付けた作者の上品なユーモアにある。これは何気ない会話ながら、親子の情愛にあふれ、平川英語の白眉と言えよう。小さい子の言葉であるから、言うことが単純なのがよい。このような言葉も英語で言うとなると大変である。右ページの日本文を見ながら自分の英語で言って見よう。「どこ行ってたの」などの表現も、学校英語では相当の力があっても、なかなか言えない。このような簡単なことを繰り返し言って身につけるのが英語を話す早道である。

A Goat

Track-03

Mom: **Wow! Where have you been all this time?**

Taro: **I was at Ichiro's house talking to his brother.**

Mom: **Really?**

Taro: **Ah h'm, and he said he would give me a goat.**

Mom: **Are you sure he said that?**

Taro: **Yes, and it's the cutest thing, eating paper and everything.**

Mom: **So you asked for it, right?**

Taro: **No, he asked me if I wanted it. So I said yes.**

Mom: **I don't know about this.**

Taro: **Sure, you can ask him.**

Mom: **Well, what do you have to give him in return?**

Taro: **I'm going to give him a puppy when it's born.**

Mom: **But what if he doesn't like dogs?**

Taro: **Oh, he likes them a lot. He told me so.**

Mom: **Well, I'll speak to him about it.**

Taro: **Will you, Mom? When?**

Mom: **Oh, in a few days.**

Taro: **Good. Don't forget, because I don't want him to change his mind.**

Mom: **But why do you want a goat so much? It's a lot of trouble to feed.**

Taro: **I don't mind it, because then I can give you a lot of good milk.**

Mom: **You mean you are going to drink it.**

Taro: **No, Mom. I've had enough milk already.**

A Goat

母　まあ、今までどこに行っていたの。

太郎　一郎君のところで　郎君の兄さんと話をしてたの。

母　あら、そうなの。

太郎　うん、そうしたら、兄さんはぼくにやぎをくれるって言ったよ。

母　本当にそう言ったの。

太郎　そうだよ。とても可愛(かわ)いくて、紙でもなんでも食べるよ。

母　それで一郎君の兄さんにせがんだのね。

太郎　ううん、兄さんがぼくに「いる？」って言ったから、ぼく「うん」って言ったんだ。

母　さあ、どうだかわからないわ。

太郎　本当だよ、聞いたっていい。

母　じゃ、その代(か)りに何をあげるつもり。

太郎　子犬をあげるんだ、今度生まれたらね。

母　でも犬が嫌(きら)いなときは。

太郎　だって、大好きだってそう言ってたよ。

母　じゃ、お母さんもお兄さんによく聞いてみましょう。

太郎　そう、お願い。いつ。

母　まあ、二三日中に。

太郎　わかった。忘れないでよ、お兄さんがいやだなんて言い出すと困(こま)るから。

母　でも、なんでそんなにやぎが欲しいの。食べ物の世話だって大変よ。

太郎　ぼくがやるから大丈夫。そしたらお母さんにおいしいミルクをたくさん飲ましてあげるね。

母　そんなことを言って、飲むのは太郎の方でしょう。

太郎　ううん、ぼくはもうお母さんのをたっぷり飲んだから。

Dialog Two

A Goat

Point 1

Mom: **Wow! Where have you been all this time?**
Taro: **I was at Ichiro's house talking to his brother.**
Mom: **Really?**
Taro: **Ah h'm, and he said he would give me a goat.**
Mom: **Are you sure he said that?**
Taro: **Yes, and it's the cutest thing, eating paper and everything.**

Wow「おや、まあ」驚きを表す感嘆詞。

Where have you been?「どこへ行ってたの。」帰ってきたばかりの人には、過去形で Where were you? でなく、現在完了形で言うことに注意。

all this time「今までずっと。こんなに長い間」

Where have you been all this week?

Where have you been all day?

I was at ... talking to ...「…に行って…に話していた」

I was at the library studying.

I was at the airport waiting for my plane to leave.

「私は空港で出発便を待っていた。」

he said he would give me「彼は私にくれると言った」He will ... が He said の後につくと、he would ... となる。

He said he would be late tonight.

I told her I would be at Ichiro's house.

the cutest thing「とってもかわいい」このような最上級は気持ちを込めて言うときに使う。 thing は creature（人）のこと。

Their daughter is such a sweet thing!

「あそこのお嬢さんはとっても可愛い。」

She's beautiful. She's the loveliest thing.

He is not feeling well, poor thing.「かわいそうに」

Point 2

Mom: **So you asked for it, right?**
Taro: **No, he asked me if I wanted it. So I said yes.**
Mom: **I don't know about this.**
Taro: **Sure, you can ask him.**
Mom: **Well, what do you have to give him in return?**
Taro: **I'm going to give him a puppy when it's born.**

asked for it「それをお願いした」この場合、for という前置詞を忘れないこと。

I'll ask you for it when the time comes.
「時が来たらあなたにお願いします。」

asked me if ...「…かどうかたずねた」ここでも時の一致を練習しよう。

He asked me if I needed more money.
I asked her if she wanted to buy it.

I don't know about this. これは文字通りの意味ではなく、「さあ、どうだか」といった感じの言い方。イントネーションによって気持ちが伝わるので、感じを出して言ってみよう。これは次の言い方についても同じである。

Sure, you can ask him.「あなたが彼に尋ねてみてもよい。」この can は may と同じ。Sure. は略式語で「いいとも」

Sure, I can do that.
「ええ、私がやってもいいよ。」
Sure, you can come tomorrow.
「ええ、あす来てもいいよ。」

to give him in return「代わりに（お礼に）やるのに」

She gave me a poem in return.
「お礼に歌を書いてくれた。」
You can give her some flowers in return.

Point 3

Mom: **But what if he doesn't like dogs?**
Taro: **Oh, he likes them a lot. He told me so.**
Mom: **Well, I'll speak to him about it.**
Taro: **Will you, Mom? When?**
Mom: **Oh, in a few days.**
Taro: **Good. Don't forget, because I don't want him to change his mind.**

what if ...「もしも…ならどうするか」

What if they don't like Japanese food?

「和食が嫌いだったらどうしよう。」

What if no one speaks Japanese?

「日本語をわかる人がいなかったらどうしよう。」

I'll speak to him about it.「私が彼にそのことで話してみよう。」

I'll speak to her about it myself.

「彼女には自分で話します。」

I spoke to her about it on the phone.

「彼女と電話で話した。」

in a few days「二三日中に」

I'll call you back in a few days.

「数日中にこちらから電話します。」

I'll read it in a few weeks.

change his mind「彼が気持ちを変える、彼の気が変る」

I changed my mind and went to see him.

I don't want him to ...「彼に…してもらいたくない」

I don't want you to disturb me.

「邪魔してもらいたくない。」

I don't want you to drive so fast.

I don't want you to call me after 10 o'clock.

Point 4

Mom: **But why do you want a goat so much? It's a lot of trouble to feed.**

Taro: **I don't mind it, because then I can give you a lot of good milk.**

Mom: **You mean you are going to drink it.**

Taro: **No, Mom. I've had enough milk already.**

Why do you want ... so much? いろいろ換えてみよう。

Why do you want money so much?

Why do you want candies so much?

It's a lot of trouble to ... 「…することはなかなか面倒だ」

It's a lot of trouble to feed pets.

It isn't a lot of trouble to go abroad. （海外旅行）

I don't mind it. 「私はそれをいやとは思わない。」

I don't mind working for him.

「彼の下だったら喜んで働きます。」

I don't mind speaking to him.

「彼には私が話してやってもいい。」

You mean ... 「…ということか」

You mean you are going to do it yourself.

You mean you saw him there.

I've had enough milk. 「ミルクは十分飲んだ。」現在完了形で言って、自分はもう飲み終えたという感じを出したもの。なお、I've had enough. は料理を腹一杯たべたときの「もうたくさんです」にも、また、あまりにもごたごた言われて「もうたくさん。うんざりだ」などという時にも使う。

Would you like some more?

No, thanks. I've had enough.

Don't tell me anymore. I've had enough.

実力チェック　　**英語で言ってみよう！**

1. 小鳥を飼(か)うのは大変だよ。
2. もうみかんはたくさんいただきました。
3. そのことは私があなたの先生にお願いしてみましょう。
4. なんでそんなにパソコン (computer) が欲しいの。
5. 総理大臣 (prime minister) はできるだけのことはすると言った。

カムカム英語と私たち

少年の頃

國吉丈夫

夕日で空が赤く染まるころ、家の裏の樫の木の垣根に身を寄せて、私はその時間を待つのであった。「カムカム エヴリバディ…」お隣の家のラジオから、証城寺の狸ばやしのメロディーにのった、明るく歯切れのよい英語の歌が聞こえてくる。そして流れるような調子で明るく親しく語りかけて、平川唯一先生は声色を巧みに使い、生き生きと英語の会話を展開させる。私は、もう一言も聞きもらすまいと集中するのであった。

音源まで 20 メートルはある。田舎の夕暮れ時とはいえ、鶏や馬の鳴き声一つで音は掻き消されてしまう。いつの間に気がついてくれたのであろうか。垣根にへばりついてじっと耳を傾ける 15 歳の少年のために、おばさんは音量を一段と大きくしてくれていたのであった。

こうして 2 年半ほど経った時である。街の教会で無料の英会話教室が始まるという。胸を躍らせて出席し、驚いた。なんと金髪の先生の英語が全部わかるではないか！ こんな嬉しいことがあろうか。土曜日はこの教室とバイブルクラスに出て 8 時過ぎに帰るという生活がそれから何年か続くことになる。

夕焼けの空をバックに、からすの群れを見上げながらの孫とのやりとり、「みんなお山に帰るのね」「そうだよ、山のおうちにね」といった英語の会話がいまも私の耳に聞こえてくる。

（くによし・たけお／千葉経済大学教授。大学英語教育学会理事）

夏目教授の試験問題

第五高等学校記念館には夏目金之助教授が英国留学のため熊本を引き上げる直前に行ったガリ版刷りの英語試験問題が展示されている。1番が単語、2番が熟語、3～6番が英文解釈で、June 27, 1900 Natsume. とサインされている。1の (1) が mastication (咀嚼) であることは、将来を予知させるが、和訳問題のうち3問には学生へのメッセージを伝えよ うとするかのような意気込みが感じられる。上のは、「人生賛歌」を引きつつ偉人の名声は永遠であり茨の冠もついには後光となって輝くと説く。下のは、恋と友情の苦悩を知らずして忠良なる臣、孝行な子たりえずと述べる文である。

- **Great men may die as well as others; but their fame lasts as long as the world. "Let us, then, be up and doing, with a heart for any fate!" If our grey hairs are crowned with thorns, let us console ourselves by thinking that they will surround us in good time with a halo of light, brighter than that which the old masters delighted to paint around the heads of the saints.**

- **He who cannot feel the intoxicating pangs of love and friendship can never be a loyal subject and an affectionate child. He is destitute of that holy flame which being indestructible comes from heaven and returns to heaven.**

Dialog Three

I LIKE EVERYTHING

みんな大好き

これは太郎が叔父さんにおごってもらう話である。レストランか喫茶店(きっさてん)かの店先で入り口のメニューを見ながらの会話であるが、陳列棚(ちんれつだな)を見ていると思ってもよい。今の飽食(ほうしょく)の時代には想像もできないが、あの頃アイスクリームひとつがどんなご馳走(ちそう)だったことか。当時の子供たちは、この夢のような話を、生つばを飲み込みながら練習したのである。

Dialog Three

I Like Everything

Track-04

Uncle: Are you tired now, Taro?

Taro: No, I'm just thirsty, that's all.

Uncle: Are you? Then, let's drink something somewhere.

Taro: How about that place over there?

Uncle: Well, let's go and see. Mmm ... There are all kinds of things. What will you have?

Taro: Oh, anything will be all right.

Uncle: Now, don't be afraid. Say what you want.

Taro: Anything you like will be all right with me.

Uncle: Shall we have some ice cream and coffee, then?

Taro: Yes. That suits me fine.

Uncle: Are you sure you don't want anything else?

Taro: No, Uncle Akio.

Uncle: What do you know about that! You are so different from your sister.

Taro: Am I? In what way?

Uncle: For one thing, she is never afraid to say what she wants.

Taro: Well, I'm not afraid, either.

Uncle: Then, why not say it like a man?

Taro: I will, if that's all right with you.

Uncle: Sure it's all right.

Taro: Then I want that ice-cream soda and shortcake.

Uncle: OK, I'll get them for you.

Taro: Wait a minute, Uncle Akio. There is something more.

Uncle: What do you mean?

Taro: I think I like everything in the store.

Dialog Three

I Like Everything

叔父　どうした、疲(つか)れたか、太郎君。

太郎　ううん、のどはかわいたけど。

叔父　そうか。じゃ、どこかで何か飲もう。

太郎　あそこはどう。叔父(おじ)さん。

叔父　さあ、行ってみよう。ほほう、いろいろあるな。太郎君は何にするかい。

太郎　ぼく、何でもいいや。

叔父　そう遠慮(えんりょ)しなくてもいいよ。好きなものを言ってごらん。

太郎　おじさんの好きなものでいい。

叔父　じゃ、アイスクリームとコーヒーにするか。

太郎　うん、ぼくそれでいい。

叔父　ほかに欲(ほ)しいものはないんだね。

太郎　ええ、大丈夫。

叔父　なんだ、太郎君は姉さんとはだいぶ違うな。

太郎　そう。どんなところが。

叔父　第一、姉さんは欲しいものははっきり言うよ。

太郎　そりゃ、ぼくだって言えないことはないけど。

叔父　じゃあ、男らしく言ってごらん。

太郎　いいの、言っても。

叔父　かまわないとも。

太郎　じゃ、ぼく、アイスクリームソーダとショートケーキもほしいな。

叔父　よしわかった、じゃ、それをもらおう。

太郎　待って、おじさん。まだあるんだ。

叔父　ほほう、何だい。

太郎　ぼくね、あそこに出てるもの、みんな大好き。

I Like Everything

Point 1

Uncle: **Are you tired now, Taro?**
Taro: **No, I'm just thirsty, that's all.**
Uncle: **Are you? Then, let's drink something somewhere.**
Taro: **How about that place over there?**
Uncle: **Well, let's go and see. Mmm ... There are all kinds of things. What will you have?**
Taro: **Oh, anything will be all right.**

I'm just thirsty.「のどが渇いただけ。」just は「ちょっと…なだけ」

I'm just sleepy.

I'm just busy now.

That's all.「それだけのこと。」

I just wanted to make sure, that's all.

「確かめたかっただけ。」

I just went to see her, that's all.

Let's drink.「飲みましょう。」これと似た言い方で、Let's have a drink. と言うと、その語感からして、ビールやワインなど酒類を飲みましょうということになる。

How about that place over there?「あの向こうの所はどうですか。」簡単なようで、日本語からは出てこない言い方。

How about that handsome boy over there?

How about that blue one over there?

What will you have?「何にしますか。」と聞くときの決まり文句。ここでは will を使うことに注意。

What will you have, Taro?

I'll have *ramen* (*tendon* / *zarusoba*).

What will you have, Mari?

I'll have spagetti.

Point 2

Uncle:	**Now, don't be afraid. Say what you want.**
Taro:	**Anything you like will be all right with me.**
Uncle:	**Shall we have some ice cream and coffee, then?**
Taro:	**Yes. That suits me fine.**
Uncle:	**Are you sure you don't want anything else?**
Taro:	**No, Uncle Akio.**

Don't be afraid.「こわがらなくてよろしい。遠慮しないでね。」

Don't be shy.

Say what you want.「何が欲しいか言いなさい。欲しいものを言いなさい。」

Take what you want.「欲しいものは持って行きなさい。」

Buy what you need.「必要なものは買いなさい。」

... will be okay with me. この場合、will が入ることと、前置詞 with を使うことに注意。

Tomorrow will be okay with me.

This blue bag will be okay with me.

Shall we have ...?「…にしようか」

Shall we have *tempura*?

That suits me fine.「それで結構です。」

Are you sure ...?「本当に…ですか」

Are you sure you locked the door?

anything else「ほかに何か」anything や something や nothing のときは、修飾するものは必ず後に付けること注意。

Don't you want anything else?

I have nothing else.

I have something else to do.

Uncle Akio 日本語は「叔父さん」と言えばそれで良いが、英語では Uncle だけでは不自然だから、必ず名前も付けて言う。

Point 3

Uncle:	**What do you know about that! You are so different from your sister.**
Taro:	**Am I? In what way?**
Uncle:	**For one thing, she is never afraid to say what she wants.**
Taro:	**Well, I'm not afraid, either.**
Uncle:	**Then, why not say it like a man?**
Taro:	**I will, if that's all right with you.**

What do you know about that!「やあ、驚いた。」これは驚いたときの決まり文句だから、このまま覚えるほかない。

different from「とは違う」

Kyoto is quite different from Osaka.

I'm a little different from my brother.

In what way?「どんなふうに」「どんな点が」

In what way is Kyoto different from Tokyo?

In what way are you different from your brother?

for one thing「一つには」「早い話が」

For one thing, I like the atmosphere.（雰囲気）

For one thing, he likes all sorts of sports.

if that's all right with you「もしあなたさえよかったら」この場合も、前置詞 with に注意。

I'll stay if that's all right with you.

Everything is OK with me.

What's the matter with you?

why not say it「言ったらどうですか」

Why not do it now?「今したらどうですか。」

like a man「男らしく 」相手が女性の場合は Why not have the guts to say it? となる。have the guts to は「…する勇気を持つ」

Point 4

Uncle:	**Sure it's all right.**
Taro:	**Then I want that ice-cream soda and shortcake.**
Uncle:	**OK, I'll get them for you.**
Taro:	**Wait a minute, Uncle Akio. There is something more.**
Uncle:	**What do you mean?**
Taro:	**I think I like everything in the store.**

Sure「それはもう、ぜったい」といった感じの副詞。

Sure you can eat it.

Sure I'll do it for you.

ice-cream「アイスクリームの」アイスクリームだけのときはハイフンなしに ice cream と書くが、後に何かがつくとハイフンをつける。

I like vanilla ice cream.

We have an ice-cream freezer.

I'll get them for you.「取ってあげよう。買ってあげよう。持ってきてあげよう。」この言葉は、上のようにいろいろの意味になるが、そのどれであるかは前後の言葉で判断する。

There is something more.「もっとあります。」こんな日本語を英語で言おうとすると、この There is ... という言い方は出にくいもの。

What do you mean?「どういうことですか。」聞き返すときの決まり文句。

everything in the store「店にあるものはみんな」

I want everything in the restaurant.

I want one of everything in the store.（ひとつづつ）

I need something that's in there.

実力チェック　　英語で言ってみよう！

1. 一つには、ここの気候 (climate) が気に入っています。

2. うどんにしましょうか。

3. どういうことですか。

4. 男らしく欲しいものを言ってごらんよ。

5. 50 年前の日本語は今のとは少し違っています。

Dialog Four

THE STUDY OF SLEEP
朝寝の研究

今朝は太郎が眠り（ねむ）の法則（ほうそく）を話題にしている。ここには文法的には現在完了形が出てくる。これをすらすら言えるようにすることは受験勉強と直結（ちょっけつ）している。受験生は家族英語を丸覚えすれば、英文も覚えられるようになる。すると英作文力が倍増（ばいぞう）する。会話力は作文力である。インスタント作文力である。これがないと挨拶（あいさつ）以上の英語会話はできない。われわれが目指すのは、自分の専門とすることを外国人と英語で議論できる力であり、家族英語はその確実な第一歩を保証する。

The Study of Sleep

Track-05

Dad: Come on, Taro. Snap out of it. It's past six.

Taro: Wait a minute. I'm thinking about something.

Dad: Well, you don't need to do that in bed, do you?

Taro: I do, because it's important.

Dad: That's no way to settle anything important.

Taro: But this is different. I have to have an answer before I can get up.

Dad: What is the question anyway?

Taro: It's this, Dad. Before dinner you are hungry, aren't you?

Dad: Why, naturally.

Taro: But after dinner you don't want to eat anymore.

Dad: That's because you're full.

Taro: Then why is it that I'm not sleepy in the evening?

Dad: And that you want more sleep in the morning?

Taro: Yes, after having slept all night.

Dad: H'm ... I never thought about it that way.

Taro: It's funny, isn't it?

Dad: That's because the law of eating is different from the law of sleeping.

Taro: Well, what is the law of sleeping?

Dad: It's like pushing a heavy wagon.

Taro: In what way?

Dad: It's always hard to start moving, but once you start it, it's hard to stop.

Taro: Oh, I see. Now, I've learned something.

父　さあさあ太郎、早く起きないともう６時過ぎだよ。

太郎　ちょっとまって。考えることがあるから。

父　なにも寝ていて考えることはないだろう。

太郎　だってこれ、とても大事なことなんだもの。

父　そんな格好で大事なことが考えられるものかね。

太郎　でもこれは特別。この答えを考えなくちゃ起きられないの。

父　その問題というのは何だね。

太郎　それはこうなんだ。ご飯の前は誰でも腹ぺこになるでしょう。

父　そりゃ、当り前だよ。

太郎　でも、ご飯がすむと、もう食べたくないのね。

父　そりゃもう、お腹が一杯だから。

太郎　じゃ、夕方はどうして眠くないんだろう。

父　そして朝になると眠いと言うんだね。

太郎　そう、一晩中寝た後なのに。

父　うーん…それは思ってもみなかったね。

太郎　とてもおかしいでしょう。

父　それは食べることの法則と寝ることの法則とは違うからだよ。

太郎　寝ることの法則ってどんなの。

父　それはまた重い車を引っぱるようなもんだ。

太郎　どうして。

父　初め動かすまでは難しいが、いったん動き出すとなかなか止まらないだろう。

太郎　ああ、分かった。それで一つ勉強ができた。

Point 1

Dad: **Come on, Taro. Snap out of it. It's past six.**
Taro: **Wait a minute. I'm thinking about something.**
Dad: **Well, you don't need to do that in bed, do you?**
Taro: **I do, because it's important.**
Dad: **That's no way to settle anything important.**
Taro: **But this is different. I have to have an answer before I can get up.**

Snap out of it.「さっさと起きなさい。」決まり文句だから、すぐ覚えて使うこと。

You don't need to do that.「そんなことをする必要はい。」

You don't need to say that.
「そんなこと言わなくていいでしょう。」
You don't need to buy that.

in bed「寝たままで」

That's no way to ...「そんな…方をするものではない」

That's no way to hit a ball.
「そんな球の打ち方をするものでない。」
That's no way to cook rice.
「ご飯はそんなに炊くものでない。」
That's no way to speak to your boss.

have to ...「…しなければならない」

I have to have a car.
「どうしても車がないといけない。」
I have to eat before I can go.
I have to work before I can watch TV.
「勉強してからでないとテレビは見られない。」

Point 2

Dad: **What is the question anyway?**
Taro: **It's this, Dad. Before dinner you are hungry, aren't you?**
Dad: **Why, naturally.**
Taro: **But after dinner you don't want to eat anymore.**
Dad: **That's because you're full.**
Taro: **Then why is it that I'm not sleepy in the evening?**

anyway「とにかく」

What do you want anyway?

Why did you do that anyway?

Why, naturally.「そりゃ、あたりまえだよ。」このような Why は「なぜ」ではなく、「まあ」というような言葉。書くときは、必ず、コンマをつける。

Why, it's you, Taro!

「やあ、太郎君じゃないか。」

don't want to ... anymore「もう ... したくない」こりごりしたときにこう言えばよい。

I don't want to go there anymore.

I don't want to study anymore.

I don't want to see him anymore.

That's because ...「 それは…だからです」

That's because you are tired.

That's because your car is new.

Why is it that ...?「…というのはどうしたわけですか。」

Why is it that you didn't bring your book?

Why is it that Japan is exporting so much?

「どうして日本はこんなに輸出するのですか。」

Point 3

Dad: **And that you want more sleep in the morning?**
Taro: **Yes, after having slept all night.**
Dad: **H'm... I never thought about it that way.**
Taro: **It's funny, isn't it?**
Dad: **That's because the law of eating is different from the law of sleeping.**

And that ... これは前の文の Why is it ... からつづくときの言い方。二つのことを言うとき は、2 番目のことの 前に必ず and that を付けて言う。

He says he worked all day and that he is sleepy.

He says he just got home and that he is hungry.

After having slept all night「一晩中、眠った後で」これは after you have slept all night と書き換えることができる。現在完了形は「眠りから覚めたばかりなのに」という感じを表す。

Do you want to sing more after having sung all day?

「一日中歌っていたのにまだ歌いたいの。」

that way「そんなふうには」反対は this way「こんなふうには」。

I never looked at things that way.

「物事をそんなふうに見たことはありませんね。」

I never thought about Japan that way.

「日本のことをそんなふうに考えて見たことはない。」

I did it this way.

「それはこんなふうにやったのです。」

different from ...「…とは違う」

Tea is different from coffee.

Udon is different from noodles.

People are not so different from each other.

Point 4

Taro: **Well, what is the law of sleeping?**
Dad: **It's like pushing a heavy wagon.**
Taro: **In what way?**
Dad: **It's always hard to start moving, but once you start it, it's hard to stop.**
Taro: **Oh, I see. Now, I've learned something.**

What is ... like?「…はどのようなものですか。」

What is his wife like?
「奥さんはどんな方ですか。」
What is your new teacher like?
What is your hometown like?

heavy wagon「重い車」というときは car より wagon がよい。

In what way?「どのような点で」

Once you start it「動き出したら」

Once he begins, he never quits.
「彼は一度始めると決してやめない。」
Once she starts shopping, she buys a lot.

I've learned something.「何か習った。いい勉強になった。」現在完了形は過去のことではなくて、たった今終わったような時にいう言い方。これに慣れることは、会話能力のステップアップの大きな山である。こんな短い文を口まねしていれば、知らない間に覚えてしまえるはずである。

We've played a lot today.
「今日はたっぷり遊んだね。」
You've worked all day today.
It's been rainy all day.

実力チェック　　**英語で言ってみよう！**

1. ちょっと待ってね。いまお茶を飲んでるから。
2. お金を少し (some money) もらわないと出かけられないのよ。
3. それはのどが渇(かわ)いているからですよ。
4. それは考えてもみなかったわ。
5. 人の一生は重き車を押すが如(ごと)し。

カムカム英語と私たち

アンクル カムカムの思い出

降旗健人

平川先生の声を初めて聞いたのは、昭和24年ごろだったと思う。それからは、夕方の6時半になると必ずラジオの前で英会話を教えていただいた。そのうちに近所の本屋さんに頼んでメンバー募集のちらしを配ってもらい、中学生から大学生までの仲間が週1回集まるようになった。こうして「カムカムを学んでアメリカへ行こう」という意味でゴーゴー支部と呼称した。

同じ世田谷区にお住まいの平川先生を数人の仲間と恐る恐るお訪ねして以来、私は地方の大会にまでお供するようになり、英語だけでない全人格的なものに感銘を受けた。私にとって最も忘れ難い恩人の一人が平川先生である。

おかげで英語をしゃべることに苦労しなくなった。慶應大学英語会から米国留学、伊藤忠商事入社。そして40年。その間、外国資本と日本企業の提携プロジェクトに携わり、国際通信会社を経営してこれた。

私の一生を振り返ってみると、その根源にはいつも平川先生がおられる。あの日、先生の放送に魅せられなかったならば、私の一生は全く異なったものになっていたと思う。平川先生の英語に出会えたお陰で、アメリカへの留学も出来たし、伊藤忠時代はいすゞーゼネラル モーターース社との提携、セブンイレブンの日本への導入、衛星メーカーのHuges Aircraft社との衛星合弁事業(現スカパー) 等のprojectに参画出来たし、伊藤忠退任後は欧米の通信会社とトヨタ自動車と組んで国際デジタル通信（株）の経営の責任者になる事が出来た、と振り返っている。

(ふるはた・たけと／元伊藤忠商事副社長、元国際デジタル通信社長)

Rabbit and Tortoise

平川唯一訳詞

Come, come, Tortoise, Tortoise dear,
Why on earth are you so slow?
There is no one like the kind of you
Walking slowly, so slowly.

What's that you said, good Rabbit dear?
Then to a race do I challenge you.
Let us run to the yonder hill.
See who'll win this, you or I.

Rush and hurry the tortoise may,
All day long he's sure to take.
Here I stop for one short rest,
Sleepy, sleepy, I'm sleepy.

O dear, what's the matter! I've overslept.
Run fast, run fast, hurry must I.
How late are you, good Rabbit dear!
Did you not say you'd win the race.

Dialog Five

FATHER'S BIRTHDAY
お父さんの誕生日

　これは自分の誕生日も忘れている父親と、今日だけは早く家に帰ってねと念を押す娘との会話になっている。今でも、夕食の時間までには帰宅できないサラリーマンは多いから、それだけでもこれは微笑ましい話題である。ところがこの話は作者にとっては特別な意味があった。昭和22年2月、これが放送された週に、1902年生まれの平川先生は45歳の誕生日を迎えた。アメリカではリンカーンの誕生日とヴァレンタインの日にはさまれた13日がこの誕生日であった。そしてまた、この月は、この番組が始まってから一周年で、最初からの聴取者はカムカムベイビーとして一歳の誕生日を迎えた。この話の結びの言葉には、こうして二重の意味が込められていたのである。

Dialog Five

Father's Birthday

Track 06

Mari: **Congratulations, Dad! Happy birthday to you!**

Dad: **Thanks, Mari. Well, this is a surprise!**

Mari: **Surprise? Why?**

Dad: **Because I had almost forgotten it myself.**

Mari: **You did! But I didn't.**

Dad: **How did you remember?**

Mari: **Well, yesterday was Lincoln's Birthday, and tomorrow is Valentine's Day, right?**

Dad: **That's right.**

Mari: **And your birthday comes right in between, on February thirteenth.**

Dad: **So that's how you remembered! You'll have to teach me how to remember yours.**

Mari: **Oh, mine is easy, because it's April Fool's Day.**

Dad: **That's true. I never thought of that.**

Mari: **Anyway, Dad, be sure to come home early tonight.**

Dad: **All right, but why?**

Mari: **Because we are going to have a big surprise for you.**

Dad: **Really? What?**

Mari: **I won't tell you now, but Mom and I have been planning it for some time.**

Dad: **So it's secret, huh?**

Mari: **Well, in a way, yes.**

Dad: **OK then, I'll just rush home tonight and find out what's up.**

Mari: **There's one thing I might tell you.**

Dad: **And what's that?**

Dialog Five

Father's Birthday

真理　お父さん、おめでとう。誕生日おめでとう。

父　ありがとう。いや、これは驚いたね。

真理　驚いたって、なぜ。

父　だって自分でも忘れるところだったよ。

真理　そお、でも私は忘れないわ。

父　どうして覚えているの。

真理　だって昨日はリンカーンの誕生日だったし明日はバレンタインでしょう。

父　うん、そうだ。

真理　それでお父さんの誕生日はちょうどその間の２月13日なんでしょう。

父　なるほど、そういうふうに覚えていたんだね。真理ちゃんの誕生日の覚え方も教えてもらっておかないといけないね。

真理　私のは簡単よ。だってエイプリルフールの日なんだから。

父　本当だ。それは気が付かなかったねえ。

真理　とにかく今日はきっと早く帰ってね。

父　わかったよ。だがなんで。

真理　とてもびっくりさせることがあるの。

父　そうかい。何だろうね。

真理　それは言いっこなし。だけど私とお母さんで前から計画していたの。

父　それでこれは秘密というわけだね。

真理　ええ、まあ。

父　じゃあ、よし。今日はひとつ大急ぎで帰って来るとしよう。

真理　たった一つだけ言っておいてもいいわ。

父　というのは。

Mari: **You'll have only one candle on your birthday cake.**

Dad: **Only one! Well, if you are short on candles ...**

Mari: **No, Dad. You are only one year old as a "Come Come" baby.**

Point 1

Mari: **Congratulations, Dad! Happy birthday to you!**

Dad: **Thanks, Mari. Well, this is a surprise!**

Mari: **Surprise? Why?**

Dad: **Because I had almost forgotten it myself.**

Mari: **You did! But I didn't.**

Dad: **How did you remember?**

Mari: **Well, yesterday was Lincoln's Birthday, and tomorrow is Valentine's Day, right?**

Dad: **That's right.**

Mari: **And your birthday comes right in between, on February thirteenth.**

Congratulations!「おめでとう」必ずsが付くことに注意。これは努力して成功したことを祝うという意味の動詞congratulateから来たものであるから、合格したときとか、入学や卒業のとき、賞をもらったときなどに言う。結婚式のときは使わないが、これは花嫁は努力して獲得するものではないという考え方があるためである。同じ「おめでとう」でも英語では、クリスマスにはMerry Christmas!、正月にはHappy New Year!と言う。

This is a surprise!「これは驚いた。」決まり文句。

had almost forgotten「ほとんど忘れていた。」過去完了形になっているのは、言われた時までは忘れていたから。

I had forgotten about it till he called me.
「彼が電話をくれるまでそのことは忘れていた。」

真理　お父さんの誕生日のろうそくは一本しかないの。
父　たった一本かい。ろうそくが足りないんだったら…
真理　そうじゃないの。お父さんはカムカムベイビーとしてはやっと一つなんだから。

Point 2

Dad: **So that's how you remembered! You'll have to teach me how to remember yours.**
Mari: **Oh, mine is easy, because it's April Fool's Day.**
Dad: **That's true. I never thought of that.**
Mari: **Anyway, Dad, be sure to come home early tonight.**
Dad: **All right, but why?**
Mari: **Because we are going to have a big surprise for you.**

that's how you remembered!「ああ、そうやって覚えていたのか。」年号を語呂合わせで覚えるのもこれである。

That's how I remember my telephone number.

That's how I got it.「そうやって手に入れたのよ。」

You'll have to teach me.「あなたは教えなければならない。ぜひ教えてもらいたい。」

You'll have to come to my house some day.

「いつかぜひ遊びに来てください。」

how to remember「覚え方」

You'll have to teach me how to dance.

You'll have to teach me how to grow roses.

「ばらの育て方を教えてくださいね。」

be sure to ...「必ず…する」

Be sure to be on time.「時間厳守だよ。」

Be sure to turn off the gas.

Point 3

Dad: **Really? What?**
Mari: **I won't tell you now, but Mom and I have been planning it for some time.**
Dad: **So it's a secret, huh?**
Mari: **Well, in a way, yes.**
Dad: **OK then, I'll just rush home tonight and find out what's up.**

I won't tell you now.「今は教えない。」こんな言い方になれることが自然な会話には大切。

I won't do it now.
I won't buy it now.
I won't eat it now.

have been planning「準備をしてきた」ずっと継続してやっているときは完了進行形を使う。

We've been planning for the wedding.
I've been driving for about ten years.

for some time「かなり前から」

I've been jogging for some time.
I've been playing tennis for some time.

in a way「言わば、ある意味では」これも英語独特の表現だから、単語の意味からはおよそ遠いことに注意。

rush home tonight「今日は大急ぎで帰る」日本語では「今夜は早くかえるよ」でも「今日は早く帰る」でもいいが、英語では、仕事を終えてから帰宅するのは today でなく tonight が普通。

what's up「何が起こるか」

What's up?「どうしたのか。何だ。」
What's up with her?

Point 4

Mari: **There's one thing I might tell you.**
Dad: **And what's that?**
Mari: **You'll have only one candle on your birthday cake.**
Dad: **Only one! Well, if you are short on candles ...**
Mari: **No, Dad. You are only one year old as a "Come Come" baby.**

one thing I might tell you「言ってもよいことが一つ」

might は may の過去形だが、このようなのは文法的には仮定法である。
仮定法で言うと、感じが柔らかくなるので、会話ではよく使われる。

This is a secret, but I might tell you.
「これは秘密だが、君には言っておいてもよい。」
I might tell you a little secret.
I might show you a picture of my grandson.

short on「足りない」

We are short on money.
We are getting short on meat and vegetables.
Japan is short on oil.

ついでに、(run) short of を使っても同じことが言える。

We've run short of oil.「ガス欠だ。」
We were running short of food.
「食料が不足しかけていた。」
We are short of staff at present.
「人員が不足している。」
I was short of breath after climbing the hill.
「その丘を登って息切れしていた。」

実力チェック　　**英語で言ってみよう！**

1. 自分でも忘れるところだった。
2. どうして思い出したの。
3. ああ、そうやって彼に連絡した (contact) のですか。
4. 私たちが前から計画してしていることが一つだけあります。
5. お米が切れてきたわ。

カムカム英語と私たち

岡村桂介

平川先生とカムカム英語

毎夕、6時になるとラジオから流れる「カムカム英語」のメロディーに心を躍らせ、慌ててテキストをめくる時代を今も懐かしく思い出します。

中学生になり、教科書の英語には興味が湧かず、そんな時、カムカム英語の存在を知りました。ラジオを聴いて、初めて英語の楽しさを実感しました。

私の父は千葉県の当時は小さな街の4代目の開業医で、病院前の大通りを隔てたところに親戚の家があり、その頃は電力状況も悪く、度々の停電の時は親戚の家でラジオを聴かせてもらいました。そんな事は苦とも思わせないほど、カムカム英語の楽しさにのめり込んでいました。

そうなると面白いもので、本物のアメリカ人に言葉が通じるか試したくなりました。2時間近く電車に乗り、日比谷公園でアメリカ兵にテキストを見せながら身振り手振りで会話を試みました。その結果は哀れなものでしたが、自信と勇気が込み上げてきました。

当時のテキストは新聞を八つ折りにしたようなものでしたが、私にはとても大切で、また貴重なものでした。街の小さな本屋さんでは扱ってもらえず、思い切って直接平川先生にその旨をご相談したところ、その後1年以上にわたり、無償でテキストを送ってくださいました。そんなご恩が実を結び、私が医大生になった際には、ロックフェラー研究所所長の通訳として抜擢され、またニューヨークの病院でインターンとして働けるという、またとないチャンスに巡り会うことができました。

東京で50年間開業医を勤めてきましたが、海外からの多くの患者様も紹介されて診療してきました。

私の人生は「平川先生の生きた英語・カムカム英語」から成り立っていると言っても過言ではありません。そしてこの英語の楽しさは自身の代で終わることなく子や孫へと脈々と引き継がれています。

平川先生とカムカム英語には感謝と尊敬の念が尽きません。「生きた英語の楽しさ」を有り難うございました。

(おかむら・けいすけ／東京OBクリニック院長)

カムカム英語と私たち

山川浩司

カムカムイブニングの思い出

疎開先から東京に戻った1946年の春でした。ラジオ放送が情報や娯楽の拠りどころだった時代、毎夕6時にNHKの第一放送にスイッチを入れると、「証誠寺の狸囃子」のメロディにのせて、「カムカム エヴリバディ」の合唱と、平川唯一先生の優しく親しみを感じる声で「カムカム レッスン」が始まりました。お馴染みなおとぎ話や唱歌にわかり易く素晴らしい訳詞をなされ、ラジオの合唱に合わせ共に歌ったものです。「兎と亀の競争」も、「カムカム トータス トータス ディア…」と。日常会話に即する英訳歌詞で、直ぐに覚え、口ずさんでいました。そして「カムカム レッスン」によって英語に親しみを感じるようになりました。

青山学院中等部以降も、英語への興味は益々強くなり、当時の進駐軍放送WVTR局の音楽番組も傾聴し、英語と米国文化への憧れと親近感が一層大きくなりました。

1958年に伝手を通じ、ニューヨークの米国籍の会社にて2年間、貿易の仕事に従事し、その後ニューハンプシャー州の器械メーカーとの合弁会社を東京に設立し、25年間その会社の経営に携わりました。振り返ると、「カムカム英語」は、外国人と通じ合える「生きた英語」を身につける「原点」でした。

それから約30年後、ラジオの声のみならずご自身に接することができたのは、東京ローンテニスクラブでした。先生は、いつもご常連の4人でメンズダブルスをなさっていました。先生の独特なサービスのスタイルは今でも鮮明に記憶しています。プレイ終了後、愛車のモーリスマイナーを駆ってクラブより去られる姿を見ながら、つい、私は「兎と亀の競争」の唱歌を、もちろん平川先生の訳詞で、口ずさんでいました。

「カムカム先生、有り難うございました。」

（やまかわ・こうじ／マーケム株式会社　元代表取締役会長）

Dialog Six

A GIANT HOME RUN
大ホームラン

上の学年のクラスと野球の試合をするなどということは、もうなくなったのかもしれない。野球は戦後の何もないときから子供のスポーツとして流行(りゅうこう)したものである。「ホームランをかっとばす」なんて英語はどういうのかなという興味を持って、やってみよう。

なお、この話は、ラジオテキスト第１号からのもので、原題は「太郎と母」。この号は最初の週の話題は、父が太郎を起こしてラジオ体操をする話。次は庭で花を植えている花子と父の対話。第３週がここで取り上げるもので、最後が一家でのかるた大会となっている。

A Giant Home Run

Track-07

Taro: **Hi, Mom!**

Mom: **Hi, Taro! You are early today.**

Taro: **Yes, Mom. I ran all the way from school.**

Mom: **You did? What for?**

Taro: **Take a guess.**

Mom: **Hum-well, I give up.**

Taro: **All right then. But first I want a glass of water.**

Mom: **A glass of water! On a cold day like this?**

Taro: **Yes, I'm thirsty.**

Mom: **OK, here you are.**

Taro: **Thanks.**

Mom: **Boy, you are really sweating!**

Taro: **Boy, that water was good.**

Mom: **Now, tell me why you came home in such a hurry.**

Taro: **Hasn't Mari come home yet?**

Mom: **No, not yet.**

Taro: **I'm not surprised.**

Mom: **Why do you say that?**

Taro: **Because she lost the game.**

Mom: **What are you talking about?**

Taro: **The baseball game. See, her class and mine had a game this morning.**

Mom: **And Mari's class lost?**

Taro: **Yes, and her class has bigger boys than mine.**

Mom: **Well, I should think so. Her class is a year older than yours.**

Taro: **And they all thought the game was a cinch.**

太郎　お母さん、ただいま。
母　お帰り。今日は早いこと。
太郎　うん、ぼく学校からずっと走ってきたんだ。
母　あらそう。どうして。
太郎　当ててごらん。
母　そうね、わからないわ。
太郎　じゃあいいや。けど先に水一杯ほしいな。
母　水ですって。こんな寒い日に。
太郎　そう、ぼくのどカラカラ。
母　じゃあ、はい、お水。
太郎　ありがとう。
母　おやおや、汗をかいてまあ。
太郎　ああ、おいしかった。
母　でもなんでそんなに大急ぎで帰ったの。
太郎　姉さんはまだ。
母　ええ、まだよ。
太郎　そうだろうと思った。
母　なんでそんなこと言うの。
太郎　だって姉さんは試合に負けたんだもん。
母　それ、いったい何のこと。
太郎　野球のことさ。ね、ほら、姉さんの組とぼくの組が試合をしたの、今朝。
母　で、真理の組が負けたんですって。
太郎　そう、それも姉さんの組の子はぼくらよりずっと大きいんだから。
母　そりゃそうでしょうとも。あの組は一年上なんですもの。

太郎　だから姉さんたちは絶対に負けるはずないって思っていたんだ。

Mom: **How did they lose it?**
Taro: **They didn't until the very end.**
Mom: **What happened then?**
Taro: **Oh, you should have seen it, Mom. I went out and hit a giant home run.**

Point 1

Taro: **Hi, Mom!**
Mom: **Hi, Taro! You are early today.**
Taro: **Yes, Mom. I ran all the way from school.**
Mom: **You did? What for?**
Taro: **Take a guess.**
Mom: **Hum-well, I give up.**

Hi, Mom. Hi は Hello の俗語。英語では、「ただいま」も「お帰り」も Hi! でよい。出かけるときは、「行ってきます」も「行ってらっしゃい」も Bye!、または Bye, bye! で良い。

all the way「ずっと」似た言い方を一緒に覚えよう。

I ran all the way from school.（ずっと）
most of the way（ほとんど）/ part of the way（途中一部分）

You did?「本当？ あらそう？」

I walked all the way from home. — You did?
I hit a home run. — You did?
I went there in a hurry. — You did?

What for Why とほぼ同じ（「なんで」と「なぜ」の違い）。

What did you do that for? = Why did you do that?

Take a guess.「当ててみて。」というときの最も普通の言い方。guess は動詞では「想像する、当てる」

I give up.「負けた。降参。お手上げ。」次の文に "Take a guess." "I give up." と続けてみよう 。

Why are you so happy? / Who came to see me?

母　それがまたどうして負けちゃったの。
太郎　最後の最後までは負けていなかったよ。
母　それでどうなったの。
太郎　お母さんに見せたかったなあ。ぼくが出て行ってホームランをかっ飛ばしたんだ。

Point 2

Taro: **All right then. But first I want a glass of water.**
Mom: **A glass of water! On a cold day like this?**
Taro: **Yes, I'm thirsty.**
Mom: **OK, here you are.**
Taro: **Thanks.**
Mom: **Boy, you are really sweating!**
Taro: **Boy, that water was good.**

a glass of water 水が欲しいときは、必ず a glass of water または some water と言い、I want water. とは言わない。

I want　a glass of milk.
　　　　a cup of tea. / a bottle of beer.

Here you are. 何かを差し出すときに言う決まり文句。お釣りを渡すときでも、郵便を渡すときでも、料理を出すときでも使う。

Here you are. This is a gift from us.

Here you are. You can open it later.

Boy! 驚きや軽蔑や喜びを表す言葉。男の子という意味はない。

Boy! Is he still in bed?　「まあ、まだ寝てるの」
Boy! What a mess!　「まあ、きたないこと」
Boy! It's terrible.　「まあ、ひどい」
Boy! What a surprise!　「まあ、驚いた」
Boy! What a shame!　「まあ、恥ずかしい」
Boy! What a fine day!　「まあ、いいお天気」
Boy! This is really good.　「うん、おいしいなあ」

Point 3

Mom: **Now, tell me why you came home in such a hurry.**
Taro: **Hasn't Mari come home yet?**
Mom: **No, not yet.**
Taro: **I'm not surprised.**
Mom: **Why do you say that?**
Taro: **Because she lost the game.**
Mom: **What are you talking about?**
Taro: **The baseball game. See, her class and mine had a game this morning.**

tell me ... 質問をするときに相手の注意を引く言葉。

Now tell me　why you ran all the way home.
　　　　　　why you went there yesterday.

lost「負けた」。「勝った」は won。

Waseda lost the game to Keio last Sunday.
Waseda won the game to Keio today.

See, その次に何かを説明しようとするときに、先ず相手の注意を引く決まり文句。日本語の「ねえ」にあたる。You see. の略。

You see,　my father is coming home today.
　　　　　I have some money today.
　　　　　Ichiro hit two home runs.

mine = my class. 英語では同じ語の繰り返しを避けて「私のもの」という意味の mine を使う。

Is that yours?　—　No, it isn't. It's hers.
Is this ours?　—　No, it isn't. It's his.

had a game「試合をした」

We had a meeting at 3:00 this afternoon.
I had a date with Jane.

Point 4

Mom: **And Mari's class lost?**
Taro: **Yes, and her class has bigger boys than mine.**
Mom: **Well, I should think so. Her class is a year older than yours.**
Taro: **And they all thought the game was a cinch.**
Mom: **How did they lose it?**
Taro: **They didn't until the very end.**
Mom: **What happened then?**
Taro: **Oh, you should have seen it, Mom. I went out and hit a giant home run.**

bigger「より大きい」

My apple is bigger than yours.

Yours is bigger than ours.

I should think so.「それはそうでしょうね。」こんな決まり文句は、何度も何度も繰り返して覚えること。独り言を言ってみよう。

till 時間的に「…まで」。同じ「まで」でも、その意味によって英語の形が変る。

I waited for her till ten o'clock.	「10 時まで」
How far is Kobe?	「神戸まで」
He can count up to a hundred.	「100 まで」
He lived to be ninety years old.	「90 まで生きた」

You should have seen it.「あなたはそれをみると良かった（見せたかった）」これには言葉ではとても言い表せないという意味が含まれている。

You should have watched that TV program.

You should have come to the party.

なお、You should have ... は決まった言い方なので、発音はひとまとまりにユシュッダブのようになる。

実力チェック　**英語で言ってみよう！**

1. さあ、どうぞ。
2. 駅からずっと歩いてきました。
3. こんな暑い日にはビールが一杯欲(ほ)しいなあ。
4. そりゃそうだろうね。なにしろ金持ちなんだから。
5. あなたもマドンナのコンサートに行けばよかったのに。

カムカム英語と私たち

胸のすく語り口

愛甲 晃生

昭和25年春、熊本県立人吉(ひとよし)高校に入学すると語学部に入部した。これは毎日昼休みには部室に集まり、前日放送分の復習をするクラブであったが、先輩の指導は他学科にも及(およ)び、多大の恩恵(おんけい)を受けた。

当時、ラジオの芸能番組では広沢虎造(とらぞう)の浪曲(ろうきょく)「清水次郎長伝」が人気をさらっており、私はその大ファンであった。虎造の魅力(みりょく)は歯切れのよい、胸のすくような語り口にある。この点、カムカムおじさんと共通している。ともに聴く者を虜(とりこ)にしてしまう魔力(まりょく)をもっている。

高校卒業時、アメリカ人とならかなりしゃべれる程度の英会話力を身につけていた。慶應(けいおう)大学から昭和33年に丸紅飯田(まるべにいいだ)に就職。入社後最初の出張のとき、偽米ドル使用の容疑(ようぎ)でハンブルグ警察に連行され長時間の尋問(じんもん)を受けたが、会話力のおかげで窮地(きゅうち)を脱(だっ)した。

過日、熊本大学に福田教授を訪ね、炎天下(えんてんか)、連れ立って『草枕(くさまくら)』ゆかりの峠の茶屋を探訪(たんぼう)した。その日は38度8分の猛暑(もうしょ)であった。山路を下りながら考えた。虎造を聴けば気が晴れる。話ができれば容疑が晴れる。先輩があれば見物ができる。とかくに人の世は住みやすい。と漱石(そうせき)先生を偲(しの)んでいると、山石に足を滑(すべ)らせからだがゆれた。額(ひたい)から汗が飛び、口からカムカムが飛び出した。「オーボーイ イツ ダーンド ハット」

（あいこう・てるお／元丸紅商事部長）

東のクラーク　西のジェインズ

徳富蘇峰は、札幌農学校のクラークと熊本洋学校のジェインズをもって、明治上期の外国人教師の東西の横綱と称している。東のクラークはわずか1年しか勤務しなかったのに、別れに際し、Boys, be ambitious! という名文句を残し、これが「少年よ、大志を抱け」という名訳になって教科書に載ったために、全国にその名を知られるようになった。西のジェインズは神風連の乱を避け、誰にも知られないように去ったため、その名を知る人は地元にも少ない。だが、知名度の低さにもかかわらず、ジェインズの功績は決してクラークに勝るとも劣るものではない…。

ジェインズの業績は英語教育の面からだけ見ても驚嘆すべきものであった。ジェインズ方式は、一年間の集中方式で何ができるかを示している。そしてすべての教科を英語を使って教えるということで、留学しなくても留学同様の成果をあげることができることを示している。必要が生んだこの教え方は、他では真似のできない実験を行ったことにもなる。今かりに優秀な生徒を選抜した中学一年生を対象に、英語を使って英語だけを教えれば、2年生から生徒はすべての教科を英語で学ぶ学力が備わることをジェインズの実績は示している。

（福田昇八著　『語学開国』大修館書店から転載）

Dialog Seven

A NEW RAINCOAT

新しいレインコート

昔は、風邪を引くと誰でも白いマスクをかけて外出したものである。これは他人に風邪をうつしてはいけないという心掛けであった。その後、そのききめが疑問視されて、この習慣はすたれていたが、最近はまたマスクをかけるようになった。早くマスクなしの世の中になることを切に願う。

A New Raincoat

Track-08

Mari: **How do you like my new raincoat, Mom?**

Mom: **Fine. That's just the right color for you.**

Mari: **Thanks. Glad you like it.**

Mom: **But you look so different in that raincoat.**

Mari: **Do I? Well, that explains everything.**

Mom: **What do you mean? What does it explain?**

Mari: **Nothing very important, but it was the funniest thing I ever saw.**

Mom: **Well, what was it?**

Mari: **You know how it is. The train was crowded, and I was being pushed around this way and that.**

Mom: **Nothing strange in that.**

Mari: **And when the car stopped with a jerk, I nearly fell.**

Mom: **You have to be careful.**

Mari: **Then the man sitting in front of me stood right up and said, "Won't you have a seat?"**

Mom: **How kind of him!**

Mari: **And who do you think that was?**

Mom: **Search me.**

Mari: **It was Dad, carrying that old briefcase.**

Mom: **No kidding! Did you say "Hello" to him?**

Mari: **I couldn't, because just then I was pushed violently from behind.**

Mom: **But didn't Dad see you?**

Mari: **He did, but he didn't seem to know me at all.**

Mom: **How funny! He must have been thinking of something.**

真理　ねえ、お母さん、どう新しいレインコート。

母　いいわね、色合いもちょうどよく合ってるよ。

真理　あら、嬉しい、お母さんにほめられるなんて。

母　でも、そのレインコート着ていると見違えるようよ。

真理　あら、そう。ああそれでわかった。

母　それ何のこと。わかったって、何が。

真理　別にたいしたことじゃないの。でもあんなにおかしかったことってないわ。

母　まあ何のことなの。

真理　それがね、電車が混んでいて、あっちへ押され、こっちへ押され、もうさんざんだったの。

母　いつだってそうよね。

真理　すると電車が急に止まってもう転びそうになったの。

母　用心しないとねえ。

真理　そのとき私の前に座っていた男の人がすっと立ち上がって、「どうぞ」って言ってくれたのよ。

母　まあ、親切な人ね。

真理　それはいったい誰だと思う。

母　わからないわ、そんなの。

真理　それがね、あの例の鞄を下げたお父さんなの。

母　あら、そうお！　それで挨拶したの。

真理　それがだめだったの。ちょうどそのとき、後ろからすごく押されたの。

母　でもお父さんはあなたを見なかったの。

真理　見たわよ、でも全然知らん顔なの。

母　おかしいのね。きっと何か考えごとでもしていたんでしょう。

Mari: **I thought so, too. But now I know it was because of this new raincoat and a mask I had on.**

Point 1

Mari: **How do you like my new raincoat, Mom?**
Mom: **Fine. That's just the right color for you.**
Mari: **Thanks. Glad you like it.**
Mom: **But you look so different in that raincoat.**
Mari: **Do I? Well, that explains everything.**
Mom: **What do you mean? What does it explain?**

How do you like ...?「…はどう思いますか。」

How do you like your new job?
How do you like the weather?

just the right color for you「あなたにぴったりの色」色合いの違いは shade というが、それも含め color を使ってよい。

That's just the right size for me.
10:30 is just the right time for me.

Glad you like it. 日本語では、こんなのを言う習慣はないが、英語では、人から服装、髪形、持ち物、料理など何のことでもほめられたときには、たいていこう言って答える習慣になっている。

What a beautiful suit! — Glad you like it.
I like your shoes. — Glad you like them.

look so different「とても違って見える。別人のようだ。」

in that raincoat「そのレインコートを着ると」英語では「着る」という意味を in で表すことに注意。

You look so nice in that blue coat.
He looked so handsome in that uniform.

That explains everything.「それが全部を説明する。それで分かった。」こんな言い方ができれば、英会話も一人前。

What do you mean? 聞き返すときの決まり文句。

真理　私もそう思ったんだけど、いま考えてみるとこの新しいレインコートを着て、マスクをかけていたかららしいわ。

Point 2

Mari:	**Nothing very important, but it was the funniest thing I ever saw.**
Mom:	**Well, what was it?**
Mari:	**You know how it is. The train was crowded, and I was being pushed around this way and that.**
Mom:	**Nothing strange in that.**
Mari:	**And when the car stopped with a jerk, I nearly fell.**
Mom:	**You have to be careful.**

the funniest thing I ever saw「見たこともないほどのおかしなこと」形容詞の最上級の後に I ever ... と言う。

It was the best movie I ever saw.
It was the most interesting story I ever read.

You know how it is.「ほら例によって。」この言葉には別にこれというほどの意味はなく、次に言うことの前置きであるから、このまま覚えておくこと。

I was being pushed around.「押し廻されていた。」

I was being chased around.「追い廻されていた。」
I was being watched by everybody.

this way and that「あっちこっち」

I walked around this way and that.

Nothing strange in that. 前に There is が省略された言い方で「そんなの珍しいことではない。」in that に注意。

with a jerk「急に、がくんと」

The taxi stopped with a jerk.

I nearly fell.「もう少しで転ぶところだった。」

I nearly fell off.「落ちるところだった。」
The project nearly fell through.（失敗寸前）

You have to be careful.「用心しなければならない。」

Point 3

Mari:	**Then the man sitting in front of me stood right up and said, "Won't you have a seat?"**
Mom:	**How kind of him!**
Mari:	**And who do you think that was?**
Mom:	**Search me.**
Mari:	**It was Dad, carrying that old briefcase.**

man sitting in front of me「私の前に座っていた人」

Won't you have a seat?「どうぞおかけください。」次の言い方もある。

Have a seat, won't you?

Won't you sit down?

Please sit down.

How kind of him!「なんて親切なんでしょう。」

How sweet of him!

How nice of you!

Who do you think that was?「それは誰だったと思うか。」do you think を疑問文の中に入れた言い方ができるようになると英会話力もかなりのものと言える。

Who do you think gave me this ring?

Who do you think came to see you?

What do you think I got?

What do you think he gave me?

Which do you think is wrong?

When do you think they will arrive?

Search me. 俗語で I don't know. と同じ意味。私をいくら探しても答えは見つかりませんよ、の意味から。

old briefcase old は必ずしも「古い」ではなく、「例の、あの、見慣れた、なつかしい」といった意味。

Point 4

Mom: **No kidding! Did you say "Hello" to him?**
Mari: **I couldn't, because just then I was pushed violently from behind.**
Mom: **But didn't Dad see you?**
Mari: **He did, but he didn't seem to know me at all.**
Mom: **How funny! He must have been thinking of something.**
Mari: **I thought so, too. But now I know it was because of this new raincoat and a mask I had on.**

No kidding!「あらまあ、本当なの、冗談じゃないの。」昔は For Heaven's sake! などと言ったが、今は使わない。

I got up at six this morning. — No kidding!
She gave me some money. — No kidding!

just then「ちょうどそのとき」

Just then the lights went off.

seem to know「知っているらしい」

He seems to know you.
He doesn't seem to know you.

not ... at all「全然…ない」ただし、Not at all. と言えばお礼を言われたのに対することばで、「どういたしまして」。

I didn't see her at all.
I didn't buy anything at all.

Didn't Dad see you? こんな言い方に慣れるのが会話上達の秘訣である。

Didn't you go there?
Didn't you speak to him just then?
Didn't you look different in that black raincoat?
Didn't the car stop with a jerk?

He must have been thinking of something.「なにか考えていたにちがいない。」

You must have been thinking of her.
drinking too much.

because of「…のために」

I couldn't sleep because of the noise outside.
The concert was cancelled because of rain.
We came home early because of her cold.
I was up till ten o'clock because of homework.

had on「かけていた（マスク）」have ... on は wear と同じ。

She had a silk scarf on.
a yellow suit on.

実力チェック　**英語で言ってみよう！**

1. ああ、それで理由（わけ）が分かった。
2. そんなこと別に何でもないでしょう。
3. あなたのお父さんってやさしいのね。
4. おまえのことなんかあの人は全然知らないようだったよ。
5. 彼は彼女に長電話していたに違（ちが）いない。

Dialog Eight

THE NOBEL PRIZE
ノーベル賞

戦後4年目の昭和24年(1949年)、湯川秀樹博士に日本人として初めてのノーベル賞が授与された。まだ戦災復興に励んでいた国民にとって、日本人の学問的業績がこうして国際的に認知されたという意義は計り知れないものがあった。日本人も世界一になったというのが庶民の感覚であった。小学校や中学校でも、「アインシュタインの相対性理論と関係ある物理学でのことらしい。相対性理論が分かる人は日本には数えるほどしかいないらしい」などと話し合ったものである。このニュースには当時の青少年を奮い立たせるものがあった。平川先生は早速これをとりあげ、題材としたのである。

The Nobel Prize

Track-09

Taro: **Wait, Dad. Don't burn that.**

Dad: **Why not? It's an old paper.**

Taro: **See what it says in it, though.**

Dad: **Wha ...? Oh, "Dr. Yukawa Receives Nobel Prize". Is that what you mean?**

Taro: **Yes. And I want to save that paper.**

Dad: **Good for you! We must remember this day of days for all Japanese.**

Taro: **And for me particularly.**

Dad: **For you? Why?**

Taro: **You remember, don't you, the school exercises last year?**

Dad: **Yes. Oh, you mean your recitation? Ha, ha, that was pretty bad.**

Taro: **I had stage fright, just like Dr. Yukawa.**

Dad: **Did he have stage fright, too?**

Taro: **That's what it says, and something more.**

Dad: **For instance?**

Taro: **He was always first in his class in school.**

Dad: **And so are you, aren't you?**

Taro: **And I have the habit of thinking about a lot of things in bed.**

Dad: **No wonder you sleep late in the morning.**

Taro: **But Dr. Yukawa figures out hard problems in bed, too.**

Dad: **Still it doesn't say he always sleeps late.**

Taro: **Well, anyway, I have a pretty good chance of getting the Nobel Prize, right?**

太郎　あ、ちょっと、それ燃やさないで。

父　どうして。古新聞だよ。

太郎　でも、書いてあることをよく見てよ。

父　うっ、ああ、「湯川博士にノーベル賞授与」これのことか。

太郎　そう、それでぼく、その新聞とっておきたいんだ。

父　そうだ。この輝かしい日を日本人として忘れてはいかん。

太郎　そしてまた、特別ぼくにとっては。

父　特別って何が。

太郎　覚えているでしょう、ほら去年の学芸会。

父　うん。ああお前の暗唱か。あれはひどかったね。

太郎　湯川博士と同じであがったんだ。

父　すると博士もそうだったのか。

太郎　そう書いてあるよ。そしてまだほかのことも。

父　どんなこと。

太郎　小学校のころはいつもクラスで一番だったって。

父　そういえば、お前もそうだね。

太郎　それにぼくは寝てからいろいろ考えるくせがあるの。

父　そうか、だから寝坊するんだな。

太郎　だって湯川博士だって寝てから難しいことを考えるんだってよ。

父　それにしても朝寝坊とは書いてないね。

太郎　まあ、とにかく、ぼくはきっとノーベル賞をもらうかもね。でしょう。

Point 1

Taro: **Wait, Dad. Don't burn that.**
Dad: **Why not? It's an old paper.**
Taro: **See what it says in it, though.**
Dad: **Wha ...? Oh, "Dr. Yukawa Receives Nobel Prize". Is that what you mean?**
Taro: **Yes. And I want to save that paper.**
Dad: **Good for you! We must remember this day of days for all Japanese.**

Why not?「どうしてか」というときはWhy?だが、「どうしていけないのか」という意味のときは not をつけて Why not? となる。

I don't want to eat. — Why not?
You can't go. — Why not? I'm old enough.

An old paper「古新聞」newspaper はふつう paper と言う。また paper は大学ではレポートの意味で使うこともついでに覚えておこう。

I deliver the papers.「新聞配達をしている。」
I read two papers every morning.
I have a paper due by Monday.（月曜日締切のレポート）

See what it says in it.「何と書いてあるか見なさい。」こういう言い方は日本語からは割り出せないから、特によく口慣らしをする必要がある。says は「書いてある」の意味である。最後の in it は「イニ」と聞こえるくらいに言えばよい。

See what it says in the calendar.
The schedule says there is a nonstop bus at nine.
The calendar says there's a full moon tonight.
See what I have in my hand.

You must remember「覚えておかねばならない、忘れてはいけない」
You must remember this number.
You must remember your ID number.（暗証番号）

this day of days「この輝かしい日、この記念すべき日」この this の代りに the を使って the day of days「最も輝かしい日」と言ってもよい。

Point 2

Taro: **And for me particularly.**
Dad: **For you? Why?**
Taro: **You remember, don't you, the school exercises last year?**
Dad: **Yes. Oh, you mean your recitation? Ha, ha, that was pretty bad.**
Taro: **I had stage fright, just like Dr. Yukawa.**

for me particularly「特にぼくには」語順は変えてもよい。

It is important for you particularly.

It is good particularly for me.

school exercises 外国の学校には「学芸会」にあたるものはないので、それにあたる言葉もない。適当な言葉で言って、それで分からないときは、内容を説明するようにすればよい。

pretty bad「とても悪い、ひどい」very bad と同 じような感じで使う。pretty は a pretty girl などのような「美しい」という意味の形容詞ではなく、「かなり」という意味の副詞。

The movie was pretty good.

It was pretty windy out there.

stage fright「場おくれ」舞台に立って、(緊張して) あがってしまうこと。マイクの前であがるの は、mike fright という。動詞は get でもよい。

I always get stage fright. I'm nervous.

Point 3

Dad:	**Did he have stage fright, too?**
Taro:	**That's what it says, and something more.**
Dad:	**For instance?**
Taro:	**He was always first in his class in school.**
Dad:	**And so are you, aren't you?**
Taro:	**And I have the habit of thinking about a lot of things in bed.**

That's what it says「そう書いてあるね」この言い方に慣れると、英語らしく言えるようになる。

That's what I did.

That's what he said.

That's what she gave me.

For instance「たとえば、というと」

in school「学校で、学校時代は」大学なら in college という。

She is first in her class.

I am majoring in English in college.

「大学で英語を専攻している。」

He is a new kid in town.（転校生）

so are you.「あなたもそうだ。」主語によって動詞が変るから、よく口慣らしをしよう。

Taro is in the first grade. — So am I.

Jiro is in my class. — So is Saburo.

have the habit of「…する癖がある」

I have the habit of getting up very early.

I have the habit of going to bed late.

I have the habit of sleeping late.

Point 4

Dad: **No wonder you sleep late in the morning.**
Taro: **But Dr. Yukawa figures out hard problems in bed, too.**
Dad: **Still it doesn't say he always sleeps late.**
Taro: **Well, anyway, I have a pretty good chance of getting the Nobel Prize, right?**

No wonder ...「だから…だ」

No wonder you look sleepy.

No wonder you came early today.

No wonder you are so generous.

「だからこんなに気前がいいのね。」

figures out hard problems in bed「寝てから難しい問題を解く」このfigureというのは元々「数字」という意味から、数字を計算するということ。

I can't figure it out.「さっぱり分からない。」

I can't figure out what is wrong with me.

always sleeps late「朝寝坊である」「朝寝坊」はsleepyhead、「早起き」はearlybirdというが、これらは今では会話で使わない。late sleeperとかearly riserとは言うが、普通には動詞を使う。

Dad always gets up early.

Dad always comes home late.

have a good chance of ... ing「…するかなりの可能性がある」goodは「良い」ではなく、「十分な」の意。Take good care. のgoodと同じ。下の例で「いくらかの見込みがあり」「見込みなし」の言い方を覚えよう。

You have a pretty good chance of winning the contest.

You have some chance of becoming a tennis instructor.

I have no chance of buying a super car.

実力チェック　英語で言ってみよう！

1. この本に書いてあることを読んでごらん。
2. だから眠(ねむ)たそうな顔をしているのね。
3. 私は朝が遅いのです。
4. ぼくはFMを聞きながら勉強する習慣(しゅうかん)がある。
5. あなたはいい実業家(businessman)になれそうだ。

英詩の韻律

英会話は話す内容が大事で、知的な会話には教養が要る。ここに上田敏訳で有名なブラウニング (1812-1889) の詩について英語の詩の決まりを勉強しよう。

The year's at the spring	時は春
And day's at the morn;	日は朝
Morning's at seven;	朝は七時
The hillside's dew-pearled;	片岡に露みちて、
The lark's on the wing;	揚雲雀なのりいで、
The snail's on the thorn;	蝸牛枝に這い、
God's in his heaven—	神、そらに知ろしめす。
All's right with the world.	すべて世は事も無し。

英詩の決まり第一は韻律（音節数）。各行は 5 音で書かれているが ('s は is の省略)、上田敏は 1、2 行は 5 音（5 文字）に訳し、3 行目は 7 音、4 行目から 2 倍の 10 音に訳している。

第二は脚韻。1、2、3、4 行はそれぞれ 5、6、7、8 行と韻を踏んでいる。天地創造で神は空を飛ぶものと地を這うものを造った。その一つが「ひばり」であり (on the wing は flying の意味)、「かたつむり」である (thorn は morn との韻合わせ)。この詩を 5 文字に訳せばこうなる。

時は春　日は朝　あさ七時　丘に露
雲雀飛び　蝸牛這い　天に神　すべてよし。

英語は音声から

「日本人はなぜ英語が話せないのか。どうすれば英語会話に上達できるか。」—その答えは外国語習得も母国語習得と同じと考える音声方式にあると思う。これは生活英語を使えるようになってから文字と文法に入る方式で、平川方式はまさにこれである。決まり文句を無意識に言えるようになるまで繰り返す。そしてその文の一語を換えて別のことを言う。会話上達にはこれ以外に方法はない。日常的に英語を聞き話す環境にない者が母国語のように英語を習得するには、相当の努力がいる。単調と思われることを繰り返し練習しなければならない。この意味で外国語はスポーツや音楽と同じである。基礎はすべて単調である。基礎を体に叩き込めば、話せるようになる。

わが国の学校英語でも、これまでの文法第一主義、文字中心主義を修正して、口まね、丸覚え方式にすること。これが、日本人が英語を話すようになるための秘策であるというのが、私の見解である。

それでは、再入門者はどうすればよいか。基本的には初心者と同じである。文法はどうか、どのように書くかは後回しにし、英文の文章全体を一まとめにして覚えてしまうようにする。そうすれば初心者より短期間で話せるようになるはずである。

Dialog Nine

A LIVING DOLL
生きた人形

これは初孫（ういまご）(first grandchild) の誕生を待ちわびる親の気持ちを描（えが）いたものである。忙（いそが）しかった子育てが終ると、人間には孫の顔を見る楽しみが待っている。この楽しみは向こうの人も同じらしく、We grow children to enjoy grandchildren. などという言い方をする。子育ては孫を持つため、というのであろうか。

A Living Doll

Mari: **Why, hello, Dad! I thought you were still in Kyoto.**

Dad: **Well, I stepped up my schedule to see the baby.**

Mari: **I didn't know you wanted to see the baby that much.**

Dad: **You'll understand when you are old enough.**

Mari: **Old enough to be called "Grandma", you mean?**

Dad: **That's it exactly.**

Mari: **That'll be a long time yet, thank God!**

Dad: **By the way, did you get the package I sent from Kyoto?**

Mari: **Oh, yes. Those dolls were beautiful.**

Dad: **Did she like them?**

Mari: **What do you mean, "she"?**

Dad: **The baby, of course.**

Mari: **Why, the baby hasn't come yet.**

Dad: **Hasn't come?**

Mari: **No. Momoe is still in the hospital.**

Dad: **She's certainly taking her time.**

Mari: **But how do you know it's going to be a "she"?**

Dad: **Because ... I want my first grandchild to grow up just like you.**

Mari: **Are you kidding me again?**

Dad: **Why, no. The lady next door was saying the same thing, too.**

Mari: **Was she? Why?**

Dad: **She said she wanted to borrow you for the Doll's Festival.**

Mari: **And what did you tell her?**

Dad: **I told her to wait until I have another one just like you.**

Dialog Nine

A Living Doll

真理　あら、お父さん、お帰りなさい。まだ京都だと思ってたわ。

父　いやあ、赤ちゃんが気になるので予定を繰(く)り上げてね。

真理　まあ、赤ちゃんがそんなに見たいなんて。

父　なあに、おまえも年をとると分かるよ。

真理　おばあちゃんって言われるようになればでしょう。

父　うん、そう。

真理　それはまだまだだから、いいわ。

父　それはそうと、京都から送った小包(こづつみ)は届いたかい。

真理　ああ、そうそう。きれいだったわ、あのお雛(ひな)さま。

父　どうだ、喜んだか。

真理　喜んだって、誰のこと。

父　誰って、赤ちゃんさ。

真理　ああら、赤ちゃんはまだ生まれてはしないわ。

父　なんだ、まだか。

真理　ええ、姉さんはまだ病院よ。

父　なかなかゆっくりだな。

真理　でもお父さん、どうして女の子って分かるの。

父　どうといわれても、初孫(はつまご)もおまえのように育てたいと思っているんだよ。

真理　まあ冗談ばっかり。

父　いや、本当だよ。隣のおばさんも同じようなことを言っていたよ。

真理　そう。なんて。

父　お雛さまにはおまえのこと貸してくれないかってね。

真理　それでお父さんはなんてお返事をしたの。

父　なあに、今におまえと同じようなのができるから待ってくれって言っといたよ。

Point 1

Mari: **Why, hello, Dad! I thought you were still in Kyoto.**
Dad: **Well, I stepped up my schedule to see the baby.**
Mari: **I didn't know you wanted to see the baby that much.**
Dad: **You'll understand when you are old enough.**
Mari: **Old enough to be called "Grandma", you mean?**

Why, hello, Dad!「まあ、お帰り、お父さん」Why は「なぜ」ではなく、「まあ」という感嘆詞だから、軽く言う。書くときは、必ずコンマをつける。

Why, hello, Peggy!
Why, it's beautiful!「まあ、きれいだこと。」
Why, this is really good!「まあ、おいしいわね。」

I thought you were still in Kyoto.「思った」と過去のときは、「京都にまだいる」の動詞も were と過去になることに注意。

I thought you were still a little boy.
I thought she was still in bed.
I thought we still had enough money.

I stepped up my schedule.「予定を繰り上げた。」

I stepped up my schedule to see you.
I stepped up my schedule to finish early.

that much「そんなに」that は副詞。so と同じ意味だが、会話ではよく使われる。

Do you want to play golf that much?
Do you want to go swimming that much?

when you are old enough「年をとったら」最後に enough を付けることに慣れるよう、いろいろ言ってみよう。

I want to drive a car when I'm old enough.
I want to buy a car when I'm rich enough.
I'll buy you a car when you're old enough.

Point 2

Dad: **That's it exactly.**
Mari: **That'll be a long time yet, thank God!**
Dad: **By the way, did you get the package I sent from Kyoto?**
Mari: **Oh, yes. Those dolls were beautiful.**
Dad: **Did she like them?**
Mari: **What do you mean, "she"?**
Dad: **The baby, of course.**

That's it. 「そうだ」というときの決まり文句。Exactly. だけでも「その通り」の意味で言う。

That'll be a long time yet. 「それはまだ、ずいぶん先のことだ。」日本語からは考え出しにくい言い方だから、よく練習しよう。

That'll be some time yet.
「もう少し先のことだ。」
That won't be a long time now.
「もう長いことではない。」

thank God! 「ありがたいことに、さいわい」似たような言い方に Thank Heavens! がある。アメリカの大学生がよく使う言い方に、Thank God, it's Friday. がある。この頭文字を取って TGIF というが、毎日たくさん勉強させられる大学生は、金曜日になると「やれやれ、やっと金耀日」と本当にほっとするのである。似たような言い方もついでに覚えよう。

Boy, what a beautiful day!
「わあ、いい天気だ。」
Thank God, I'm safe!
「やあ、助かった。」
Everything is ready, thank goodness!
「わあっ、準備オーケーよ。」

Point 3

Mari: **Why, the baby hasn't come yet.**
Dad: **Hasn't come?**
Mari: **No. Momoe is still in the hospital.**
Dad: **She's certainly taking her time.**
Mari: **But how do you know it's going to be a "she"?**
Dad: **Because ... I want my first grandchild to grow up just like you.**

The baby hasn't come yet.「赤ちゃんはまだ生まれていない。」日本語で考えると The baby isn't born yet. で、これでも間違いではないが、come を使うのが慣用的。アメリカでは赤ちゃんが生まれると、クリスマスカードに A baby came last October. We have a new addition to our family. と書く。「赤ちゃんが生まれる」の意味では arrive もよく使われる。

The baby arrived at five in the morning.

No. 日本語の「そうよ」が英語ではノーなのに注意しよう。日本語では、「生まれていないのか」という問に対して、「そうだ」と答えるが、英語では、答えが、（生まれて）いないなら、いつもノーである。

Has the baby come yet?　「生まれたか。」
No, not yet.　「いや、まだ。」

Hasn't the baby come yet?　「まだ生まれていないか。」
No, not yet.　「そう、まだ。」

Momoe 日本語では「（義理の）お姉さん」となっているが、英語では my sister-in-law と言わずに、名前を言うのが普通。

She is certainly taking her time.「彼女（赤ちゃん）は時間をかけている。」ホテルなどに迎えに行って、「私はロビーで待っていますから、どうぞごゆっくり用意をなさってください。」という時には、Take your time. と言えば良い。

How do you know ...?「どうして分かりますか。」

How do you know it's going to rain tomorrow?

How do you know you'll pass the exam?

"she"「女の子」ふつう男の子は boy、女の子は girl という。赤ちゃんが男か女か尋ねるときは、

Is it a boy or girl?

と言う。ついでながら、日本人はふつう「かわいい赤ちゃん」と言うが、アメリカ人は、a beautiful baby と言う（だからジョン・レノンの歌 Beautiful Boy は「かわいい坊や」と訳すのが正しい）。

grow up to be just like you「大きくなってあなたと同じようになる。」次の文の him のところにいろいろと実名を 入れて言ってみよう。

I want you to grow up to be just like Lincoln.

I want you to grow up to be just like him.

Point 4

Mari: **Are you kidding me again?**
Dad: **Why, no. The lady next door was saying the same thing, too.**
Mari: **Was she? Why?**
Dad: **She said she wanted to borrow you for the Doll's Festival.**
Mari: **And what did you tell her?**
Dad: **I told her to wait until I have another one just like you.**

Are you kidding me?「私をからかうのですか。」kid は「子やぎ」から「子供」の意味になり、動詞では「からかう」となった。

The lady next door「隣のおばさん」

The lady next door teaches English.

The man next door works at a bank.

until「まで」これは till と同じ。

Please wait here until I come back.

Wait until you are old enough.

実力チェック　英語で言ってみよう！

1. 台風 (typhoon) はまだ沖縄だと思っていた。
2. 彼女って誰のことですか。
3. どうして宅急便 (package) がまだ着(つ)いていないと分かりますか。
4. 君たちもあの選手のように育ってもらいたい。
5. またからかってるの。

Dialog Ten

A GREAT PITCHER IN THE MAKING

名投手の卵

今日の話は、大学に合格して太郎の家に下宿することになった昭夫おじさんの荷物が着いたところから始まる。昔の荷物はふとんなどを大きな布の袋に入れ厳重に紐を掛けて鉄道便で送ったもので、とてもスーツケースなどという結構なものではなく、ラジオテキストでは baggage になっていた。しかし、アメリカでは suitcase というのが普通ということで、ここではそうした。また、日本では名前は言わずに、叔父さんとか叔母さんなどというのが普通だが、アメリカでは必ず名前を付けて Uncle Bob などと言う習慣になっていることを知っておきたい。

A Great Pitcher in the Making

Track-11

Taro: **Wow, what a huge suitcase! Is it Uncle Akio's?**

Mom: **That's right. It came just now.**

Taro: **Is he coming today?**

Mom: **No. He will be here the day after tomorrow.**

Taro: **Great! I can hardly wait.**

Mom: **You're really excited to see him, huh?**

Taro: **I sure am. This time he's going to stay quite a while, isn't he?**

Mom: **Yes. He is going to live here while he goes to school.**

Taro: **Not a "school". It's a "college", isn't it?**

Mom: **Yes. He'll be a freshman.**

Taro: **Do you think he'll play with me like he used to?**

Mom: **Well, I suppose he'll be busy with his studies.**

Taro: **But he won't let me down.**

Mom: **What do you mean?**

Taro: **He said he would coach me, and make me a great pitcher.**

Mom: **That's a big order.**

Taro: **But you don't know,—I'm a pretty good pitcher.**

Mom: **Yes, except for a few broken windows.**

Taro: **Oh, that's because Kenji can't catch.**

Mom: **What a shame!**

Taro: **And Uncle Akio says I have a very good arm.**

Mom: **He said so? Then let's see if that good arm can help me carry this suitcase.**

太郎　わあっ、大きな荷物。それ叔父さんの。

母　そうよ。いま届いたの。

太郎　叔父さん、きょう来るの。

母　いいえ、あさって来るはずよ。

太郎　わあっ、待ち遠しいなあ。

母　まあ、そんなに会いたいの。

太郎　そう。今度はずっとうちにいるんでしょう。

母　そうよ。うちから学校へ通うんですもの。

太郎　学校じゃなくて大学でしょう。

母　そう、大学一年生ね。

太郎　また前みたいに遊んでくれるかな。

母　そうね、勉強が忙しいでしょう。

太郎　でも、約束は守ってくれるだろうな。

母　約束って何のこと。

太郎　ぼくをコーチして名投手にしてやるって言ったの。

母　それは大変だこと。

太郎　だって、ぼく投げるのがうまいんだよ。お母さんは知らないけど。

母　そうでしょう、時々ガラスを割るのが玉に傷（きず）だけど。

太郎　ああ、あれはけんじ君が球を受けそこねるんだもの。

母　あらまあ。

太郎　それに叔父さん言ってたよ、ぼくは肩がとてもいいって。

母　そうお。じゃ、そのいい肩でこの荷物を運ぶのを手伝ってもらいましょうね。

Point 1

Taro:	**Wow, what a huge suitcase! Is it Uncle Akio's?**
Mom:	**That's right. It came just now.**
Taro:	**Is he coming today?**
Mom:	**No. He will be here the day after tomorrow.**
Taro:	**Great! I can hardly wait.**

Wow, what a huge suitcase!「まあ、大きなスーツケースだこと。」

Wow, what a perfect day!

Wow, what a great bike!

Is it Uncle Akio's?「それは叔父さんのものですか。」最後の ...'s で「のもの」の意味になる。こんな簡単な言い方をしっかり覚えよう。次の問に That's right. It came just now. と応答してみよう。

Is this yours?

Is that mine?

Is it Jiro's?

He will be here.「彼はここに来る。」これは He will come here. よりも普通の言い方。次のような英語らしい言い方を使ってみよう。

I'll be there at ten tomorrow.

「あす 10 時にそちらへ行きます。」

I'll be with you soon.「すぐそちらへ行きます。」

I can hardly wait.「待つことができないくらいだ、待ち遠しい。」会いたくてたまらない人に一度は言ってみたい言い方。「今度はパフェ食べに行こうか。」と誘われたようなときも使って。

I can hardly wait to eat your *tempura* dinner.

I can hardly wait to take my shoes off.

Point 2

Mom:	**You're really excited to see him, huh?**
Taro:	**I sure am. This time he's going to stay quite a while, isn't he?**
Mom:	**Yes. He is going to live here while he goes to school.**
Taro:	**Not a "school". It's a "college", isn't it?**
Mom:	**Yes. He'll be a freshman.**

I sure am.「そうだよ。」これは You are excited ... に対して、Yes, I am excited. という気持ちをもっと口語的に強く表現すると I sure am. となる。なお、主語を省略した Sure am. も広く使われる（ゲーリー・クーパーがよく使った）。問いかけが Do you want to see him that much? だったら、答えはこれでは駄目で、I sure do. のようになる。

quite a while「かなりの間」

I was gone quite a while.「ずいぶん留守していた。」

It took quite a while to finish my homework.

while he goes to school「学校に行く間は」

I'll work here while you go shopping.

I'll watch the baby while you cook.

college 厳密には総合大学を university、単科大学を college と言うが、一般的に大学のことは college を使う。

He goes to college.「彼は大学生です。」

I went to college in Kyoto.

freshman「一年生」これは女子学生にも使えるが、man が男の意味なので最近は first-year student と言う。

I am a sophomore.	（2 年生）
I am a junior.	（3 年生）
I am a senior.	（4 年生）
I am an undergraduate.	（学部学生）
I am a graduate student.	（大学院生）

Point 3

Taro:	**Do you think he'll play with me like he used to?**
Mom:	**Well, I suppose he'll be busy with his studies.**
Taro:	**But he won't let me down.**
Mom:	**What do you mean?**
Taro:	**He said he would coach me, and make me a great pitcher.**
Mom:	**That's a big order.**

like he used to「前にやっていたように」この like は文法的には as を使うのが正しいが、口語では like を使う。

He used to be a heavy smoker.

He doesn't smoke like he used to.

「前のようにはたばこは吸いません。」

She used to paint a lot.

She doesn't paint like she used to.

busy with his studies「勉強で忙しい」with に注意。

Mom is always busy with a lot of things.

I'll be busy with cooking this afternoon.

let me down「私を落胆させる」let down は熟語で「がっかりさせる、裏切る」。Don't let me down.「がっかりさせないで」はアメリカの歌詞によく出るせりふ。

make me a great pitcher「名投手にしてくれる」これは投げるのをうまくするの意味。

I'll make you a good golfer.

He made her a professional golf player.

That's a big order.「それは大変だ。」a large order とも言い、「困難な仕事、無理な注文」のこと。

Point 4

Taro: **But you don't know,—I'm a pretty good pitcher.**
Mom: **Yes, except for a few broken windows.**
Taro: **Oh, that's because Kenji can't catch.**
Mom: **What a shame!**
Taro: **And Uncle Akio says I have a very good arm.**
Mom: **He said so? Then let's see if that good arm can help me carry this suitcase.**

I'm a pretty good pitcher.「投げるのがかなりうまい。」pretty は副詞で「かなり」。日本語の言い方と違うからよく覚えよう。

He is a pretty good cook.「彼は料理がとても上手です。」

She is a pretty hard worker.

except for a few broken windows「時々窓をこわすほかは、窓さえこわさなければ」

He is a great man except for his drinking habit.

「酒さえ飲まなかったら偉い人なんだが。」

What a shame!「おやまあ。なんてひどい。」

I missed my train. — What a shame!

I was late again. — What a shame!

have a very good arm「いい肩をしている」英語では、肩ではなく腕ということに注意。

The rookie has a pretty good arm.

「その新人はなかなかいい肩をもっている。」

Let's see if ...「…かどうかみてみよう。」

Let's see if you can read this.

Let's see if you can lift this stone.

help me carry「運ぶのを手伝う」

Let me help you wash the dishes.

Let me help you find your way.

実力チェック　英語で言ってみよう！

1. これはあなたのですか。
2. 待ち遠しいなあ。
3. お母さんが料理をする間、赤ちゃんはぼくがみています。
4. 父さんは歩くのがとても早い。
5. このパソコンを使えるか (use this personal computer) やってみよう。

カムカム英語と私たち

ペギー葉山

大きな宝物

「これからは英語の時代！ 英語を話せなくちゃ。このテキストが楽しそうだよ。」

会社帰りの父が駅の売店で買ってきてくれたテキストが私と平川先生のカムカム英語との出会いでした。戦争という真っ暗なトンネルからやっと抜け出した昭和21年のことです。

私の宝物ともいえる古びて赤茶(あかちゃ)けたテキストのページをひろげると、夕方6時の時報と共に聞こえてきた「カムカムエブリバディ」の歌声が、平川先生のあの歯切れのよい、流れるような英語が聞こえてきます。私はこの番組で習った英語を活用することによって一つの人生をきり開いたといっても過言(かごん)ではありません。

歌手になった私は平川先生とのご縁で本当に親しくさせていただきました。あの「南国土佐を後にして」を「マイホームトサ」と英訳していただき、颯爽(さっそう)と羽田空港を飛び立って海外公演に出かけたものでした。戦後の私たち日本人に大きな夢と希望をたくさん贈って下さった平川先生との出会いは、私の人生の大きな宝物として輝き続けることでしょう。

(ペギー・はやま／ジャズシンガー)

My Home Tosa

「南国土佐を後にして」

ペギー葉山
平川唯一訳詞

Many are the years gone by
Since I left my home
Way down south in dear old Tosa
Where my old folks stay.

Oh, how I long to hear it
Once again that lovely song
Sung so sweetly as I parted,
“Yosakoi” melody.

My heart flies to old Tosa.
For I hear you gently calling
Over the rainbow never fading
Until my dreams come true.

Dialog Eleven

FATHER'S HEADACHE

おとうさんの頭痛のたね

これは大人の会話である。日本語では、子供の言葉は大人の言葉とは全くといっていいほど違うが、英語では両者に違いはない。だから、日本語訳の方を見れば子供の言葉になっていても、それを大人がそのまま使うことができる。

Father's Headache

Track-12

Dad: **Aren't you going to bed yet, Taro? It's past eleven.**

Taro: **No, Dad. I have a long way to go yet.**

Dad: **Why don't you finish it tomorrow?**

Taro: **That's too late. Tomorrow noon is the deadline.**

Dad: **Deadline! A reporter's job isn't easy, is it?**

Taro: **No, but I don't mind. I like the job.**

Dad: **But don't work too hard, now.**

Taro: **No need to worry. But why don't you go to bed, Dad?**

Dad: **Well, there's something I have to do tonight.**

Taro: **Then we are in the same boat.**

Dad: **Exactly. I have some writing to do, too.**

Taro: **Really? What for?**

Dad: **I've been asked to be the go-between at a wedding.**

Taro: **Great!**

Dad: **Well, it's not so rosy as you think.**

Taro: **Why not?**

Dad: **I have to make a speech at the reception.**

Taro: **When? Tomorrow?**

Dad: **No, the day after.**

Taro: **Then you have all day tomorrow to work on it.**

Dad: **Yes, but then I need a day to memorize it.**

Taro: **Don't worry, Dad. They would all be happier if you forgot the whole thing.**

Dialog Eleven

Father's Headache

父　まだ寝ないのか、太郎。もう 11 時過(す)ぎだよ。

太郎　ええ、まだまだなんだ。

父　じゃ、あしたにしたらどうだね。

太郎　そうはいかないんだ。あしたの正午(しょうご)が締切(しめきり)なもんで。

父　締切！　いや、記者の仕事も楽じゃないね。

太郎　ええ、でも平気だよ、好きな道だから。

父　しかし無理をせんようにな。

太郎　大丈夫です。お父さんこそ先に休んだら。

父　それが少しやることがあるんでね。

太郎　じゃあ、ぼくと同じだ。

父　そうなんだよ。やっぱり書くのでね。

太郎　そう。何を。

父　実は結婚の媒酌人(ばいしゃくにん)を頼まれたんだよ。

太郎　やあ、それは素敵(すてき)だ。

父　ところがそれが素敵じゃないんだよ。

太郎　どうして。

父　披露宴(ひろうえん)で挨拶(あいさつ)をしなきゃならんのだ。

太郎　それはいつ。あした。

父　いや、あさって。

太郎　じゃあ、あした丸一日あるでしょう。

父　うん、だが暗記するのに一日かかるんでね。

太郎　気にしない方がいいよ。みんな忘れちゃったらかえってみんなが喜ぶでしょうよ。

Point 1

Dad: **Aren't you going to bed yet, Taro? It's past eleven.**
Taro: **No, Dad. I have a long way to go yet.**
Dad: **Why don't you finish it tomorrow?**
Taro: **That's too late. Tomorrow noon is the deadline.**
Dad: **Deadline! A reporter's job isn't easy, is it?**

Aren't you going to bed yet?「まだ寝ないんですか。」go to bedはベッドに行くと言うのではなく「寝る」という意味だから、ふとんに寝るのでも、これで良い。

I have a long way to go.「まだ（完成までには）なかなかだ。」これは慣用表現だから、ただ覚えること。最後の to go は受験英語では大学の水準だが、これも家族英語である。

Have you finished the book yet?
No, not yet. I have just started.
I have a long way to go.
I still have 300 pages more to go.
「まだあと 300 頁ある。」

Why don't you ...?「…したらどうですか。」

Why don't you do it now?
Why don't you go to bed?

deadline「しめきり」もとは囚人が、もし越えたら打ち殺されると定められた囲い線のことであるが、それが移り変わって今では新聞、雑誌などの締切の時間のことを言う。

a reporter's job「記者の仕事、記者であること」

A teacher's job isn't easy these days.
「近ごろの先生は大変だ。」
A salesman's job isn't easy.
A housewife's job isn't so easy.

Point 2

Taro: **No, but I don't mind. I like the job.**
Dad: **But don't work too hard, now.**
Taro: **No need to worry. But why don't you go to bed, Dad?**
Dad: **Well, there's something I have to do tonight.**
Taro: **Then we are in the same boat.**
Dad: **Exactly. I have some writing to do, too.**

I don't mind.「気にならない。平気だ。」これに続けて「好きですから」と言うとき、because などを前に付けない。日本語ではぶっきらぼうと思われるくらいに言えば英語では丁度良い。日本語の語尾にあたるのは英語ではイントネーションである。

I like sushi. It's great.

Don't work too hard.「働き過ぎるな。無理はしないでね。」このようなねぎらいの言葉は覚えておいて使ってみよう。

Don't study too hard.
Don't go too far.「あまり遠くへは行かないでね。」

No need to worry.「心配する必要はない」前に There is が略された言い方。

No need to send a gift.
No need to buy anything.

Why don't you ...「…したらどうですか」

Why don't you do it yourself?
Why don't you ask him?

we are in the same boat「同じ境遇だ。同じことだ。」同じ船に乗り合わせて運命を共にするという意味である。

have some writing to do「書かねばならないものがある」

I have some reading to do tonight.
I have some teaching to do tomorrow.

Point 3

Taro: **Really? What for?**
Dad: **I've been asked to be the go-between at a wedding.**
Taro: **Great!**
Dad: **Well, it's not so rosy as you think.**
Taro: **Why not?**
Dad: **I have to make a speech at the reception.**

go-between「媒酌人、仲人」外国には日本の仲人のようなのはないが、友人が仲に立って陰から結婚成立の労を取ることはある。そのような人を matchmaker という。

at a wedding「結婚式で」この at に注意。
I have to speak at a club meeting.
I had to speak at his reception.

not so rosy as you think「思うほどいいものじゃない」rosy は「ばらのような、いい」
It's not so easy as you think.
It's not so nice as you think.

Why not? 同じ「なぜ」でも、否定のときは not を付ける。
I can't go. — Why not?
I did't go. — Why not?
I won't go. — Why not?

make a speech「挨拶をする」この場合、make という語を使うことと、不定冠詞 a を使うことに注意。
I have to make a speech at the opening ceremony.
「開会式で挨拶しなければならない。」
I have to give a lecture on Hawthorne.
「ホーソンについて講演しなければならない。」
I gave a talk on bullying to the whole school.
「全校生徒にいじめについて話をした。」

Point 4

Taro: **When? Tomorrow?**

Dad: **No, the day after.**

Taro: **Then you have all day tomorrow to work on it.**

Dad: **Yes, but then I need a day to memorize it.**

Taro: **Don't worry, Dad. They would all be happier if you forgot the whole thing.**

the day after = the day after tomorrow.「あさって」日にちの言い方を練習しよう。

Let's go skiing the day after.

We went swimming the day before.「おととい」

We'll have a match a week from today.

「来週の今日、試合がある。」

We'll visit you a week from Friday.

「来週の金曜日に訪ねます。」

to work on it「仕上げるのに」

How long did you work on the book?

「その本を書くのにどれくらいかかりましたか。」

I worked on it for ten years.

We worked on the project for the whole year.

「そのプロジェクトに丸一年取り組んだ。」

I need a day.「一日かかる。」

I need a week to work on it.

I need more time to type it.

They would be all happier if you forgot「忘れたらかえって喜ぶでしょう」仮定法過去だから過去形で言うことに慣れよう。

They would be disappointed if you didn't come.

「あなたが来なかったらがっかりしますよ。」

They would all be happier if you fell asleep.

実力チェック　英語で言ってみよう！

1. もう済(す)みましたか。いや、まだなかなかです。
2. すこし休んだらどうですか 。
3. 明後日(あさって)することがあるのです。
4. コピーするのに丸一日かかります 。
5. ぼくが行かないほうが、彼等(かれら)は喜ぶでしょう。

Dialog Twelve

WHEN WE GROW UP
大人になったら

これは昭和 23 年の春休みに放送された分である。当時は電力不足ですぐに停電になるような時代で、予告なしに電気が切れ、しばらくはだまって待っているほかなかった。この討論(とうろん)会では、将来の日本を背負(せお)う若者が集まって未来の夢を語るというものであったが、現実にあの頃の若者が今は社長になり会長になっている。この討論は今となってはピンとこない内容だが、司会者の言葉や発言者の言葉などはそのまま立派に通用する。そこで先(ま)ず、このままで練習してみよう。それから、今の時代にふさわしい内容になるように自分で考えて単語を換え、新しい内容にして討論しよう。地球資源問題でも、環境保全問題でも、政治改革問題でも、英語で論(ろん)じあうときの決まり文句は同じである。このような場合の発言には独特の重みというものがあるが、これも家族英語の発展したものである。

When We Grow Up

Track-13

Chair: I am very happy that you are all here today. So let's start our discussion right away.

Mari: I believe our topic for today was, "When we grow up," wasn't it?

Chair: Exactly. So I want you all to speak up and tell us what your ideas and your dreams are.

Mari: Mr. Chairman, when I grow up, I would like to go to America and speak to Americans in fluent English.

Chair: That's splendid! But before you can do that, we must first make Japan a respectable country.

Ichiro: Absolutely! That's why I am studying so hard to become the leader of the Come Come Party.

Chair: Good for you! And how are you going to run the country?

Ichiro: First, I'm going to make a speech, saying, "Ladies and Gentlemen, let's all be friends."

Momoe: Then we'll all raise our hands and say, "Okay!"

Mari: But wait. That's all well and good for us here in Tokyo, but how about those people who are far away?

Jiro: We will broadcast it, of course. I am hoping to be an announcer myself.

Momoe: But they won't be able to hear your speech if the electricity fails.

Saburo: No problem. I will be the president of the power company and light up the whole town, using hydroelectric power.

Mari: What will you do if there's no rain, Mr. President?

Saburo: Now, that could be tough.

Chair: No, it isn't. All we have to do is to mine a lot of coal and generate electricity.

司会　きょうは皆さん、ようこそおいで下さいました。ではさっそく討論会を始めましょう。

真理　たしか今日のお題は「大きくなったら」でしたね。

司会　そうです。どうか皆さんの活発なご意見なりご希望をおきかせ下さい。

真理　私は大きくなったらアメリカへ行ってアメリカ人と上手な英語で話したいと思います。

司会　いいですね。しかしそれには先ず日本を立派な国にしなければいけないわけですね。

一郎　そのとおりです。だからぼくはカムカム党の総裁になるよう猛勉強中なんです。

司会　えらいですね。そしてどんな政治をしますか。

一郎　先ず、「皆さん、仲よくしましょう」と演説をします。

百恵　そしたら私たちがみんな「賛成」と手をあげるのね。

真理　あら、でも、そりゃ東京にいる者はそれでいいけれど、遠くの人はどうしますか。

次郎　もちろんそれは放送するんです。ぼくはアナウンサー志望ですからね。

百恵　だけど、停電したら聞けませんね。

三郎　大丈夫。ぼくが電気会社の社長になって水力発電で全国に明るい電気をつけますよ。

真理　雨が降らなくても大丈夫ですか、社長さん。

三郎　そうだな、そいつは困ったなあ。

司会　困る事はありませんよ。石炭をたくさん掘って火力発電をやればいいでしょう。

Ichiro: **Great idea! Now, who will volunteer to be in charge of coal mines?**

Momoe: **I'll cook a lot of nourishing food for the person who does it.**

Chair: **Well, our time is up. Thank you all for coming.**

Point 1

Chair: **I am very happy that you are all here today. So let's start our discussion right away.**

Mari: **I believe our topic for today was, "When we grow up," wasn't it?**

Chair: **Exactly. So I want you all to speak up and tell us what your ideas and your dreams are.**

Mari: **Mr. Chairman, when I grow up, I would like to go to America and speak to Americans in fluent English.**

I am very happy that ... 日本語の「本日はお忙しいところ、お集まりいただきまして、ありがとうございました。」にあたる。「ただ今ご紹介いただきました…です」も I am happy to be here. で良い。

So let's start ... right away.「では、さっそく…を始めることにいたしましょう。」right away は「すぐに」。

I believe our topic for today was ..., wasn't it?「本日の議題は…でしたね。」この was は is でも良いが、この「でしたね」と「ですね」の感じは日本語と同じ。

I want you all to speak up「自由に発言してください。」

Chairman 司会者は moderator とも言うが、呼びかけるときは Mr. Chairman! と言って手を挙げ、指名されてから発言することになっている。男女どちらでも chairman と呼べるが、最近は性差別を避けて chairperson 又は chair を使う。

I would like to ...「私は…したいと思います。」

I would like to own a car.

speak up in English.

一郎　そうだ、そうだ。だれか炭鉱（たんこう）の係りになってくれないかな。

百恵　そうしたらその人においしい栄養料理をしてあげるわ。

司会　では、もう時間になりました。皆さん、ありがとうございました。

Point 2

Chair: **That's splendid! But before you can do that, we must first make Japan a respectable country.**

Ichiro: **Absolutely! That's why I am studying so hard to become the leader of the Come Come Party.**

Chair: **Good for you! And how are you going to run the country?**

Ichiro: **First, I'm going to make a speech, saying, "Ladies and Gentlemen, let's all be friends."**

Momoe: **Then we'll all raise our hands and say, "Okay!"**

That's splendid!「それは結構。」相づちのことば。

a respectable country「立派な国」人から尊敬されるようなのが respectable.

He is a respectable person.

We must make our company a respectable one.

That's why ...「だから…」

That's why you speak good English. / That's why I went to Tokyo.

Good for you!「えらい。感心だ。」ほめるときの言葉。

How are you going to ...?「どのように…するつもりか」

How are you going to find the right person? / to support yourself?

run the country「国を治める」この run は manage の意。

My father runs a grocery store.

Bill runs a computer company.

Ladies and Gentlemen!「皆さん」演説の始めにいう決まり文句。女性がいないときは Gentlemen! 女性だけのときは Ladies! と呼びかける。

Let's all be friends.「仲良くしましょう。」

Point 3

Mari: **But wait. That's all well and good for us here in Tokyo, but how about those people who are far away?**

Jiro: **We will broadcast it, of course. I am hoping to be an announcer myself.**

Momoe: **But they won't be able to hear your speech if the electricity fails.**

Saburo: **No problem. I will be the president of the power company and light up the whole town, using hydroelectric power.**

But wait.「だが待てよ。でも。」

well and good「大いに結構」これは熟語。

That's all well and good for you, but how about me?

「あなたはそれでいいとして、私はどうなるの。」

I am hoping to be ... myself.「私は…になりたいと思っている。」

I am hoping to be a teacher myself.

I am hoping to be a guitarist myself.

be able to ...「…できる」

I was not able to light up the whole house.

You will be able to drive a car when you're 17.

if the electricity fails「停電になれば」fail は「失敗する」のほか、「うまく機能しない」の意味でも使う。

I failed my driving test again.

The brakes failed and he couldn't stop his car.

No problem.「問題ない。簡単だ。いいですよ。」決まり文句。

No problem. I can fix it in no time.

「簡単だ。すぐ直せるから。」

No problem. You'll get it.

「いいよ。買ってあげるから。」

Point 4

Mari: **What will you do if there's no rain, Mr. President?**
Saburo: **Now, that could be tough.**
Chair: **No, it isn't. All we have to do is to mine a lot of coal and generate electricity.**
Ichiro: **Great idea! Now, who will volunteer to be in charge of coal mines?**
Momoe: **I'll cook a lot of nourishing food for the person who does it.**
Chair: **Well, our time is up. Thank you all for coming.**

What will you do if …?「もし…なら、どうしますか。」

What will you do if she doesn't come?

What will you do if there're no tickets?

That could be tough. 直訳すれば、それは大変であり得る、という意味から、「それは大変だ。」

All we have to do is to …「…しさえすればよい。」

All you have to do is to go there.

All we have to do is to meet him.

volunteer「すすんで申し出る」

Who will volunteer to wash the dishes?

「片付けは誰がやりますか。」

Who will volunteer to drive her home?

「彼女を家まで送ってくれる人はいませんか。」

be in charge of「責任者になる」

I work in the sales department.「私は営業部です。」

Mr. Sato is in charge of the department. He is our boss.

「佐藤さんがうちの責任者で、部長です。」

Our time is up.「時間になりました。」決まり文句。

実力チェック　　**英語で言ってみよう！**

1. 先ずは7時に起きなければなりません。
2. だから私は毎日テニスをしているのです。
3. 電気が切れたらどうしますか。
4. 先生にすぐ言えばいいのよ。
5. 部屋の掃除は誰がやってくれますか。

人生賛歌

アメリカで最も有名な詩の一つはロングフェロウ（1807-82）の人生賛歌（1839）であろう。この人はボードン大学を出てヨーロッパに留学したのち、22歳のときから母校で外国語を教え、28歳でハーヴァード大学の教授に迎えられ、18年間この職にあった。この教訓詩は32歳のときの作である。

（福田昇八著『イギリス・アメリカ文学史』南雲堂による）

1

Tell me not, in mournful numbers,　悲しき歌に言うなかれ
　Life is but an empty dream!　生は空しき夢なりと
For the Life is dead that slumbers　眠れる生は死せるなり
　And things are not what they seem.　ものは見かけと違うもの。

2

Life is real — life is earnest —　生は真なり　生は実
　And the grave is not its goal:　墓が終着点ならず
Dust thou art, to dust returnest,　土なれば土にかえるは
　Was not spoken of the soul.　魂のことならず。

3

Not enjoyment, and not sorrow,　楽しみでなく悲でもない
　Is our destn'd end or way;　われらが定め行く道は
But to act, that each tomorrow　働き行きて毎日が
　Find us further than today.　一歩先へと進むべし。

4

Art is long, and time is fleeting　芸長くして時は飛び
　And our hearts, though stout and brave,　心は健く勇めども
Still, like muffled drums, are beating　覆える太鼓鳴るがごと
　Funeral marches to the grave.　打つは葬送行進曲。

5

In the world's broad field of battle	世の広大な戦場で
In the bivouac of Life,	生の露営のその地にて
Be not dumb, driven cattle!	曳かれる牛となるなかれ
Be a hero in the strife!	なれよ苦闘の英雄に。

6

Trust no future, howe'er pleasant!	楽しい明日を信ずるな
Let the dead past bury its dead!	過去には過去を埋めさせよ
Act — act in the glorious Present!	生きよ輝く現在に
Heart within, and God o'er head!	心を胸に神の下。

7

Lives of great men all remind us	偉人伝よむ者は知る
We can make our lives sublime,	気高い生をわれも生き
And, departing, leave behind us	去るとき後に残せると
Footsteps on the sands of time.	時の砂丘に足跡を。

8

Footsteps, that, perhaps another,	その足跡をまたたれか
Sailing o'er life's solemn main,	世の荒波を行く者が
A forlorn and shipwreck'd brother,	身は難破した兄弟が
Seeing, shall take heart again.	見て勇気づくことだろう。

9

Let us then be up and doing,	だから元気にがんばろう
With a heart for any fate;	命運いかにあろうとも、
Still achieving, still pursuing,	常に成し遂げ追い求め
Learn to labor and to wait.	働いて待つこと学べ。

Dialog Thirteen

PRICE FOR EVERY HOME RUN

ホームランの代償

これは少年野球団の話である。そのうちにあちこちに立派な球場ができて近所の民家に球が飛び込むこともなくなったが、戦後しばらくはどこでも近所の空(あ)き地で練習する姿が見られたものである。都会の子供たちはこの話のようなことを実際に話し合って決めて、実行していたのである。野球は、戦後の子供に手軽な喜びを与えたゲームの一つであり、人間をつくる場でもあった。

Price for Every Home Run

Track-14

Mom: I don't see you playing baseball these days. Are you tired of it?

Taro: No, but I have something more important to do.

Mom: Really? What can that be?

Taro: We are going to work hard and save up some money.

Mom: Oh, who told you to do that?

Taro: Nobody. It's our own idea.

Mom: Do you mean all the boys are going to do the same thing?

Taro: Sure, all my baseball friends.

Mom: I see, so you can buy balls and bats, h'm?

Taro: Oh, no, we are not going to buy anything.

Mom: No? That's funny.

Taro: You see, we are sure to get into trouble if we don't have enough money.

Mom: Why is that?

Taro: Because we all hit too many home runs.

Mom: But, I don't see how that can cause any trouble.

Taro: Well, every time we break a window we have to be responsible for it.

Mom: I see. That's a very good idea.

Taro: And we've decided to pay twice the price of the glass we break.

Mom: My! And how much have you saved up now.

Taro: Just enough to cover five home runs, that's all.

母　この頃ちっとも野球をしないね。もう飽(あ)きたの。

太郎　いいや、もっと大事なことがあるから。

母　あらそう。何でしょうね、それ。

太郎　ぼくたちね、一生懸命働いてお金をためるの。

母　まあ、誰がそんなことをしろって言ったの。

太郎　誰も言わないよ、ぼくたちで考えたの。

母　じゃ、ほかの子供たちも一緒なのね。

太郎　ええそう、野球の友達がみんなで。

母　ああ、わかったわ。そうしてボールやバットを買うんでしょう。

太郎　違うよ。別に何も買うんじゃないけど。

母　そうなの。変だわね。

太郎　だってお金がないときっと面倒(めんどう)なことが起(お)こるから。

母　どうして。

太郎　ぼくたちね、ホームランを打ちすぎるんだ。

母　あら、でもなんでそれがそう面倒なことになるの。

太郎　だって、窓をこわしたら、ぼくたちだって責任があるでしょう。

母　そうね。それはいいところに気がついたわ。

太郎　それで、もしこわしたら、そのたびにガラス代の２倍払うことに決めたの。

母　まあ。それでお金はもうどれくらいたまったの。

太郎　まだたったホームラン５本分だけなんだ。

Price for Every Home Run

Point 1

Mom:	**I don't see you playing baseball these days. Are you tired of it?**
Taro:	**No, but I have something more important to do.**
Mom:	**Really? What can that be?**
Taro:	**We are going to work hard and save up some money.**
Mom:	**Oh, who told you to do that?**
Taro:	**Nobody. It's our own idea.**

see you playing baseball「君が野球しているのを見る」

I don't see you playing computer games these days.

I don't see you working in the garden these days.

tired of「あきた」tired from（疲れた）と一緒に覚えよう。

Many people are never tired of playing pachinko.

I'm tired from working all day today.

have something more important to do「より大事なことがある」

I have nothing more important to do than this.

Is there anything more important to do?

What can that be?「一体なんでしょう。」What is it? より感情のこもった言い方。

What can this be?「これは何だろう。」

Who can they be?「あれは一体誰だろう。」

save up some money「お金をためる」save は「節約する、ためる」の意だが、貯金のときは up を付けて使う。

It took me several years to save up for a new car.

I am saving up 10,000 yen every month.

Who told you to do that?「誰がそうしろと言ったか。」

Nobody. 否定の相づち。事物のときは Nothing. という。

Who told you to open this box? — Nobody.

What did you do this morning? — Nothing.

our own idea「私たちが考え出した考え」our idea の強調。

That's my own idea. / That's my own car.

Point 2

Mom: **Do you mean all the boys are going to do the same thing?**
Taro: **Sure, all my baseball friends.**
Mom: **I see, so you can buy balls and bats, h'm?**
Taro: **Oh, no, we are not going to buy anything.**
Mom: **No? That's funny.**

Do you mean …?「…という意味か。」念を押すときに使う。

Do you mean this is your own violin?

Do you mean you've saved up all the money?

all the boys all the … は何にでも使える。

All the students are in class now.「授業中」

Imagine all the people living for today. (John Lennon)

Sure.「そうだとも」Yes. と同じ相づちで、会話でよく使う。

Did you read it? — Sure.

Did you tell her? — Sure.

so you can buy …「…を買えるように」これは目的を言い表す場合の型で、so で始める。文章では so that … と書く。

Open the window so you can see better.

I sat on the front seat so I could see better.

「もっとよく見えるように前の座席に座った。」

That's funny.「それは変だ。」これも相づち。

That's interesting.

That's strange.

Point 3

Taro: **You see, we are sure to get into trouble if we don't have enough money.**

Mom: **Why is that?**

Taro: **Because we all hit too many home runs.**

Mom: **But, I don't see how that can cause any trouble.**

Taro: **Well, every time we break a window we have to be responsible for it.**

You see, ...「あのね、それはね。」会話の調子をつけるのに使う。

You see, he called me last night.

「実はゆうべ彼から電話があってね。」

You see, I was driving in the rain.

we are sure to ...「きっと…する」

We are sure to win.「われわれはきっと勝つ。」

Be sure to turn off the gas.「必ずガスを消しなさい。」

You are sure to get into trouble if you don't do it now.

too many home runs too many（数えられるもの）と too much（数えられないもの）を使い分けよう。

I bought too many sandwiches.

I bought too much meat.

I have too many things to do today.

I have too much to do today.

I don't see how ...「どうして…か分からない。」

I don't see how you can get up so early.

I don't see how you can walk so fast.

that can cause any trouble「それが問題を起すもとにもなる」can は「…のこともある」の意味。

Smoking too much can be harmful to your health.

「たばこののみすぎは健康を害することがある。」

Traveling abroad can be dangerous.

every time「…するたびに」

Every time I see you, you look happy.

Every time I go, the shop is crowded.

be responsible for「…に責任がある」

I am responsible for all of you.

I am responsible for the food department.

Point 4

Mom: **I see. That's a very good idea.**

Taro: **And we've decided to pay twice the price of the glass we break.**

Mom: **My! And how much have you saved up now.**

Taro: **Just enough to cover five home runs, that's all.**

That's a very good idea.「それは大変いい考えだ。」

That's an excellent idea.

That's not a bad idea.「それも悪くないね。」

twice the price「代金の２倍」

I paid half the price.

I paid twice the price.

I paid three times the price.

I had to pay ten times the fare.（料金の 10 倍）

enough to cover「払うに十分なだけ」just をつけると「やっと十分なだけ」となる。cover は pay for に同じ。

I've saved up just enough to buy a mountain bike.

My salary is just enough to cover the family needs.

「私の給料は家族の生活費を払うのがやっとだ。」

that's all「それだけ」

I just did as you told me, that's all.

「私は言われた通りにしただけですよ。」

実力チェック　英語で言ってみよう！

1. あなたは100万円も貯めたって言うの。
2. ここの費用 (expenses) を払うくらいは持っているよ。
3. 彼がどうしてあんなに料理がうまいのかわからない。
4. いつ行ってもあの食堂は混んでいる。
5. 飲み過ぎはからだに毒です。

カムカム英語と私たち

カムカム英語と私

徳光 義人

戦後直ぐに疎開先で赤痢（せきり）にかかり長期療養（りょうよう）を余儀なくされた私に、父は自分が使った英語の教科書を使って英語の扉を開いてくれました。その後通い始めた三軒茶屋にある教会の英語教室で、カムカムクラブのGo Go支部の方々とお会いしたのがカムカムクラブとの出会いでした。同支部の最年少者として仲間に入れてもらい、Go Go支部の毎週の会合に参加しました。この会合は、平川先生の放送が終了し、Go Goの定期会合がなくなるまで続きました。

平川先生のご自宅が私の両親の家から徒歩5分ほどのところにあったため、毎回平川先生のご自宅に伺い、奥様から先生のサイン入りのテキストを購入させていただきました。また先生が放送にのぞむ際には、他のメンバーとともにNHKのスタジオに入らせていただいたことも懐（なつ）かしい思い出です。カムカム英語のイベントの一つとして、平川先生の地元、世田谷区内の全支部が共催した世田谷大会が駒澤大学の講堂で催（もよお）されたときには、プログラムの一つにあったExtemporaneous Conversation Contestというものに Go Goの先輩と組んで出場し、優勝したことも忘れがたく、誇らしい思い出です。私の英語の基礎はこうして育まれました。

東京外国語大学を卒業し、日本鋼管株式会社に就職した後も英語との縁は続きました。当時、アメリカの4大製鉄会社の一つであったNational Steelという会社に日本鋼管が投資して経営に参画することになりました。私は会社から選ばれ、NS社の上級副社長としてNS社の本社があったPittsburghに派遣されました。

経営全般につき、アメリカ人の経営者たちと7年間に渡ってアメリカ式の経営に携わり、私の人生観も多様に変化しました。

駐在中の1989年には、同市にあった日米協会の3代目会長として日米交流の促進を図るためJapan FestivalをP市と共に主催して、中曽根康弘元総理、山本七平氏、蜷川幸雄氏など各界の著名人に訪米いただき、講演、演劇をしていただきました。同時に折り紙教室などの市民レベルの交流を進めました。1991年には、日本鋼管がPhipps Conservatory（植物園）に盆栽を中心とする日本庭園を寄贈して、日米友好の一助としました。日米協会は現在も活動しています。

このような私の人生の基本となった日米経済協力や友好関係に参画できた理由は英語力であり、そのベースとなったのは平川先生の「カムカム英語」でした。もう一つ追加して申し上げると、大学時代に私の人生の良き伴侶と出会うことができたのも英語のお陰です。平川先生への感謝はいつも心に持っています。

（とくみつ・よしと／National Steel（米国）Senior Vice President）

Dialog Fourteen

SEEING HOLLYWOOD IN THREE MINUTES

3分間でハリウッド見物

これはハリウッドの健おじさんを訪ねた真理がおじさんに案内してもらう場面である。ここには身近なものをたずねたり、説明したりするときの決まり文句がいっぱいある。みんなはこれを応用して、自分の町の名所を英語で案内するときの練習をやってみよう。そのためには、まず右のページの日本語を見ながら、左の英文がすらすらと言えるようになることが第一である。おじさんはおじさんらしい貫禄のある声を出して問答をしてみるとよい。一人二役でやるときは、その人物らしい声で言ってみよう。なお、ハリウッドは平川青年がシアトルの大学を出て初めて役者として職を得た町であり、結婚した町でもあり、このおじさんの説明にも思わず熱がこもっている。palm trees の元の注には、これは「しゅろ」あるいは「やし」の類で、その種類もいろいろあるが、これが街路樹として立ち並んでいるハリウッドの町はいかにもすがすがしく、気候が暑いわけではないが熱帯的な別天地の感が深い。」とある。

Mari: **These streets are beautiful! Lined on both sides with palm trees.**

Uncle: **Yes, this is Hollywood Boulevard.**

Mari: **Where is that Griffith Park you were talking about, Uncle Ken?**

Uncle: **We are in it now. See those tennis courts? They all have lights, so you can play there in the evening.**

Mari: **What's this on the left?**

Uncle: **That's the Greek Theater, where outdoor plays and concerts are held.**

Mari: **Now, we're on top of the hill.**

Uncle: **Yes, and see that white dome over there?**

Mari: **Oh, I wonder what it is.**

Uncle: **That's the famous planetarium where interesting things are shown about the moon and stars.**

Mari: **Shall we go in there and see?**

Uncle: **No, we don't have time now, so let's hurry on.**

Mari: **Look, there is a beautiful theater, and it says Chinese Grauman.**

Uncle: **Yes. They often have the premier of Hollywood's movies there.**

Mari: **What're all those footprints on the cement?**

Uncle: **You see, they are the autographed footprints of the different actors and actresses who starred in various movies.**

Mari: **What's that big building there, Uncle Ken?**

Uncle: **That's the Paramount Motion Picture Studio.**

真理　まあ、きれいな通りだこと、両側にしゅろの木が並んで。

叔父　うん、これはねハリウッド大通りというんだ。

真理　おじさんが話していらしたグリフィス公園はどこなの。

叔父　ここがもうその公園の中なんだ。あそこにテニスコートがあるだろう。あれにはみな電燈（でんとう）がついていて夜でもやれるんだよ。

真理　この左の方にあるのはなあに。

叔父　あれはギリシャ劇場（げきじょう）でね、野外劇やコンサートをやる所なんだ。

真理　あ、もう丘の上に出ちゃったわ。

叔父　うん、ほら、あそこに白いドームがあるだろう。

真理　あら、あの中に何があるのかしら。

叔父　あれが有名な天文館（てんもんかん）でね、月や星についていろいろ面白いものがあるんだよ。

真理　じゃ、入ってみましょうか。

叔父　いや、今は時間がないから。さあ急いで行こう。

真理　あら、あそこにきれいな劇場があるわ、チャイニーズ・グローマンですってよ。

叔父　そうだ、あそこでね、ハリウッド映画の封切り（ふうぎ）上演がよくあるんだよ。

真理　あのセメントの上にあんな足跡（あしあと）がたくさんあるのは、あれなあに。

叔父　あれはね、あの一つ一つにそれぞれ映画で主役をやった俳優（はいゆう）や女優の名前が足跡に直筆（じきひつ）で書いてあるんだよ。

真理　あの大きな建物（たてもの）はなんですの、おじさん。

叔父　あれがパラマウント撮影所だよ。

Mari: **So, that's where they make those beautiful pictures.**

Uncle: **Yes. And you may have a chance to see them shoot pictures one of these days.**

Point 1

Mari: **These streets are beautiful! Lined on both sides with palm trees.**

Uncle: **Yes, this is Hollywood Boulevard.**

Mari: **Where is that Griffith Park you were talking about, Uncle Ken?**

Uncle: **We are in it now. See those tennis courts? They all have lights, so you can play there in the evening.**

These streets are beautiful! 「両側にしゅろの木が並んできれいね。」を、英語では二つに切って表現していることに注意。

This street is beautiful! Lined on one side with gingko trees.
（いちょう）

Hollywood Boulevard ハリウッドを横に貫く広い並木通り。日本の町は「何町何丁目」といったふうに一定の区画に名がついているが、アメリカの町は通りに名がついていて、その通りはどこまで行っても同じ名である。そして家の番地は1丁ごとに100の単位を加えてゆく原則になっている。

Griffith Park これはハリウッドの後ろにある山を全部公園化したもので、その広大なこと、施設の行き届いていることは他に例が少ない。

Where's the spagetti restaurant you were talking about?

Where's the handsome boy you were talking about?

so you can ... 接続詞の so は so that の略。you を主語にした言い方に慣れよう。

They have benches, so you can rest there.

They have rental shoes, so you can skate there.

真理　じゃあ、あそこであの美しい映画を作るのね。
叔父　うん、そのうちにまりちゃんも実際に撮影しているところを見る機会があるだろう。

Point 2

Mari: **What's this on the left?**
Uncle: **That's the Greek Theater, where outdoor plays and concerts are held.**
Mari: **Now, we're on top of the hill.**
Uncle: **Yes, and see that white dome over there?**
Mari: **Oh, I wonder what it is.**
Uncle: **That's the famous planetarium where interesting things are shown about the moon and stars.**

What's that ... 「…のあれはなあに」の言い方を練習しよう。
What's this on the right here? / What's that over there?

we are ... は「いま…にいる」と言うとき使う。
We're now on the fourth floor. / We're in the White House now.
We're at the bus station.

I wonder ... は「…かな」というときの決まり文句。
I wonder where he is going. / I wonder what time it is.
I wonder what he is trying to do next.

Greek Theater 昔のギリシャ劇場を現代式に改良して作った野外劇場。

That's ... where ... 案内するときの決まり文句。
That's the museum where French paintings are shown.
That's the house where Natsume Soseki once lived.
That's the pool where I often go swimming.

the famous planetarium この天文館はグリフィス公園の高い丘の上にあって、ハリウッドとロサンゼルスの全市を見下ろす絶景の地にある。

Point 3

Mari: **Shall we go in there and see?**
Uncle: **No, we don't have time now, so let's hurry on.**
Mari: **Look, there is a beautiful theater, and it says Chinese Grauman.**
Uncle: **Yes. They often have the premier of Hollywood's movies there.**

Shall we go in and see?「入って見てみようか。」go in there も同じ。

Shall we go in and eat?

Shall we go in there and rest?

We don't have time.「時間がない。」

We don't have money now.

We don't have hands now.（人手）

Let's hurry on.「急いで行きましょう。」この場合、on をつけないとただ「急ぎましょう」となるし、つければ「急いで行きましょう」という意味になる。

Look, there is ...「ほら、…がある」

Look, there is a big tower.

Look, there is a cute little girl.

it says Chinese Grauman「チャイニーズ グローマンと書いてある」say は「言う」の ほかに「書いてある」の意味にもよく使うから覚えておこう。

The sign says "No Parking."

The paper says it'll be rainy tomorrow.

The calendar says today is the summer solstice.

「カレンダーに今日は夏至だと書いてある。」

the premier「封切上演」新作映画がハリウッドで封切りされるときには、その映画に出演したスターはもちろん、他にも多くの俳優や女優が招待されるので、それを見ようとする見物客で黒山の人だかりとなる。

Point 4

Mari: **What're all those footprints on the cement?**
Uncle: **You see, they are the autographed footprints of the different actors and actresses who starred in various movies.**
Mari: **What's that big building there, Uncle Ken?**
Uncle: **That's the Paramount Motion Picture Studio.**
Mari: **So, that's where they make those beautiful pictures.**
Uncle: **Yes. And you may have a chance to see them shoot pictures one of these days.**

footprints on the cement セメントの足跡はこの劇場の呼び物で、ここで封切された映画に出演したスターのために、そのつど敷き石の一こまを抜き取り、そこへ新しいセメントを流し込み、その上にスターの足跡を印し、それに自署してもらうことになっている。

autographed footprints 日本では人にサインしてもらうというが、英語では sign は書類や手紙に署名するときに使う語で、記念のためのサインは autograph という。

The president signed his name on the agreement.
May I have your autograph?「サインをお願いします。」
I have an autographed book of the author.（サイン本）

make pictures「映画を作る」映画を撮影するのにカメラを回すのは shoot pictures、写真を写すのは take pictures と言う。

you may have a chance to see「見る機会があるかも知れない」see は姿を見るだけで、紹介されて話しをするのは meet を使う。

You may have a chance to see famous stars there.
You may have a chance to meet my parents.

one of these days「近いうちに」

I want to play tennis one of these days.
We plan to make a trip to Europe one of these days.

実力チェック　英語で言ってみよう！

1. その道は松並木でとてもきれいだった。
2. あそこは地元の物産 (local goods) が展示してあるところです。
3. あそこは酒を作るところです 。
4. 彼等はいつ日本へ来るのかな。
5. あなたは彼女がトスカ (Tosca) を歌うのを見る機会があるかもしれない。

カムカム英語と私たち

橋本徹

道はひらけた

私は中学生の頃から熱心なカムカムファンであった。かねて平川先生が郷土の大先輩と知り、先生をその郷土、高梁(たかはし)市にお招(まね)きしたいと願っていたが、昭和25年の秋、私が岡山県立高梁高等学校1年生のときこれが実現した。先生は奥様とご一緒に来訪(らいほう)された。その際、われわれは英語祭を開き、ご夫妻の前で「ヴェニスの商人」を上演した。

東京大学に進学してからは、何度か世田谷区太子堂(たいしどう)町のご自宅にお邪魔(じゃま)していろいろとご指導をいただいた。大学卒業後、直(ただ)ちに富士銀行に入行、2年後の1959年から1年間、フルブライト奨学生として米国に留学させていただいた。富士銀行では主として国際業務畑を歩かせていただき、ロンドンに6年間、シカゴに2年間勤務する機会を与えられたが、これもカムカム英語のお陰で無事任務を果たすことができた。今は亡き平川唯一先生に心からお礼を申し上げる次第である。

外国語の習得は年をとってから始めたのでは遅すぎる。頭の柔(やわ)らかい、若いうちに始めるのがベストだ。その意味で、小中学生にも親しみ易(やす)いやり方で英語会話を教えられた平川先生のご功績(こうせき)はまことに大であったと思う。私の道もこれでひらけたのである。

(はしもと・とおる／富士銀行会長)

黄水仙（きずいせん）

I Wandered Lonely as a Cloud

by William Wordsworth　　福田昇八訳

I wandered lonely as a cloud	高くただよう雲のごと
That floats on high o'er vales and hills	野越え山越えさまよえば
When all at once I saw a crowd	現れいづるひとむれの
A host, of golden daffodils;	野を埋め尽くす黄水仙
Beside the lake, beneath the trees,	池のほとりに木の下に
Fluttering and dancing in the breeze.	舞いつ踊りつそよ風に。
Continous as the stars that shine	続きゆくこと天の川
And twinkle on the milky way,	光り輝く星のごと
They stretched in never-ending line	どこどこまでも伸びゆきて
Along the margin of a bay:	水辺に沿って限りなく、
Ten thousand saw I at a glance,	一目に見ゆる幾千本
Tossing their heads in sprightly dance.	頭（こうべ）もおどる軽ろやかに。
The waves beside them danced, but they	はたの湖面もおどれども
Out-did the sparkling lines in glee:	きらめく波も比ならず、
A poet could not but be gay,	楽しからずや歌人（うたびと）も
In such a jocund company:	かくも陽気な仲間もち、
I gazed—and gazed—but little thought	見れども見れど思わざり
What wealth the show had brought:	そのもたらした富の意味。
For oft, on my couch I lie	椅子に寝そべりぼんやりと
In vacant or pensive mood,	しばし想いに沈むとき
They flash upon that inward eye	心をよぎるあの姿
Which is the bliss of solitude;	これぞ孤独の喜びよ、
And then my heart with pleasure fills	嬉しさ胸にこみあげて
And dances with the daffodils.	共に踊るよ黄水仙。

Dialog Fifteen

LOOKING FOR A JOB

面接

これは英語で就職の面接を受ける場面である。ここには英語で電話の応答をしたり、商業文を書いたりするほどの英語力を持った人が登場する。将来、外資系の事務所や航空会社の客室乗務員など、英語を使って仕事をしたいと願っている人もこれだけできるように練習しておけば大丈夫である。もっとも、いまではこの場面のように支配人が受付をしているような家庭的な事務所は少なくなったが、基本的なやり取りはここにみな含まれている。

Looking for a Job

Track-16

Toshio: How do you do! Is this the Sunrise Company?

Manager: Yes. What can I do for you?

Toshio: Well, my name is Toshio Aoki; and I saw your advertisement in the paper this morning.

Manager: Oh, yes. I'm the manager here. Have a seat, won't you?

Toshio: Thank you, sir.

Manager: I see you speak good English, but can you write business letters in English?

Toshio: Not very well, but I am studying it now, sir.

Manager: Studying it by yourself?

Toshio: No. I'm taking a course at night school.

Manager: Fine. Now, did you bring your résumé with you?

Toshio: Yes, I have it both in Japanese and English.

Manager: May I look at them?

Toshio: I hope they are all right. I wrote them in a hurry this morning.

Manager: What sort of work did you do in this construction office?

Toshio: I was in charge of books in the business department.

Manager: I see. And you quit that job this June, right?

Toshio: Yes, because, for one thing, I wanted to study English, and find a job where English is really needed.

Manager: Well, in that case, our export business here will give you all the chance you need to practice English.

Toshio: Will you give me a chance?

Manager: I don't see why not. When can you start?

Dialog Fifteen

Looking for a Job

敏夫　こんにちは。あのう、サンライズ商会はこちらでしょうか。

支配人　ええ、何かご用ですか。

敏夫　私は青木敏夫(としお)という者ですが、今朝の新聞でこちらの広告を見て参(まい)りました。

支配人　ああ、そうですか。私がここの支配人です。まあどうぞおかけ下さい。

敏夫　どうも恐(おそ)れ入ります。

支配人　英会話がよくおできになるようですが、英語の商業文のほうもおできになりますか。

敏夫　できるというほどではないので、いま勉強しています。

支配人　独学(どくがく)ですか。

敏夫　いいえ、夜学(やがく)に行っています。

支配人　それは結構(けっこう)。で、履歴書(りれきしょ)はお持ちですか。

敏夫　はい、日本語のと英語のと二通書いて参(まい)りました。

支配人　じゃ、ちょっと拝見(はいけん)しましょう。

敏夫　これでよろしいでしょうか。実はけさ急(いそ)いで書いたものですから。

支配人　この建築事務所ではどんな仕事をしておられましたか。

敏夫　営業部で帳簿係(ちょうぼがか)りをしておりました。

支配人　そうですか。で、今年の６月に辞(や)めたんですね。

敏夫　はい、一つには英語を勉強したかったためと、そして英語を必要とする仕事をしたいと思ったものですから。

支配人　そうですか、それだったら、うちの輸出業なら英語を使う機会は十分あるでしょう。

敏夫　じゃ、やらせて下さいますか。

支配人　もちろんいいでしょう。それで、いつから始められますか。

Toshio:	**Anytime you say, sir.**
Manager:	**Then report here at eight tomorrow morning.**
Toshio:	**Eight in the morning. Thank you, sir.**
Manager:	**Glad you came in.**

Point 1

Toshio:	**How do you do! Is this the Sunrise Company?**
Manager:	**Yes. What can I do for you?**
Toshio:	**Well, my name is Toshio Aoki; and I saw your advertisement in the paper this morning.**
Manager:	**Oh, yes. I'm the manager here. Have a seat, won't you?**
Toshio:	**Thank you, sir.**

What can I do for you? これは店に来た客や、事務所に来た外来者に対して言う決まり文句である。「いらっしゃいませ」「何かご用ですか」にあたる。

advertisement これは長くて言いにくいため、略して ad という俗語を使うことが多いが、面接などの場合はに、正しく advertisement と言わないと、物事に不注意な人と判定されることもあるので注意したが良い。略語好きのアメリカ人もこんな点にはきわめてきちょうめんである。

in the paper「新聞で」前置詞は in であることに注意。印刷物ならすべて in でよい。ただ、ラジオやテレビのときは on を使う。

I read it in his new book.

The news is in all papers and magazines.

I heard it on the radio. / I often watch a movie on TV.

Have a seat.「おかけ下さい。」これと同じ意味で Have a chair. / Take a chair. / Sit down. などの言い方があり、場合によっては、座る椅子を指差して Please. と低い声で言うのが非常に丁寧に聞こえることがある。

敏夫	**いつでも結構です。**
支配人	**じゃ、あしたの朝８時にここへ来てください。**
敏夫	**朝の８時、ありがとうございます 。**
支配人	**いや、ご苦労さまでした。**

won't you? = Will you not? の略。前につけて言うのも、後ろにつけて言うのも同じ。

Have some more, won't you?

「もうすこしいかがですか。」

Come in, won't you?

Thank you, sir. 英語には日本語の敬語はないが、このように sir を付けて言うことで尊敬の念を表す。相手が女性の場合は ma'm を付ける。食堂の従業員などは注文を受けてから Yes, sir.（かしこまりました）ということになっている。面接の時は、これをつけて言うと試験官に好印象を与える。

Point 2

Manager:	**I see you speak good English, but can you write business letters in English?**
Toshio:	**Not very well, but I am studying it now, sir.**
Manager:	**Studying it by yourself?**
Toshio:	**No. I'm taking a course at night school.**
Manager:	**Fine. Now, did you bring your résumé with you?**
Toshio:	**Yes, I have it both in Japanese and English.**

I see you speak good English「英会話が上手ですね」最初の I see は「…ですね」に当たる言い方。

I see you have a new car.「新車をお持ちですね。」

I see you speak good Japanese.

studying it この場合、it を忘れやすいから注意。

by yourself = alone「自分だけで」「独学で」

I went to meet him by myself. / I made it all by myself.

taking a course「勉強している」学校で１科目だけを受購しているときの言い方。２科目以上を取っているなら taking courses と言わねばならない。なお、「学校で」と言うときは in でなく at を使うことに注意。

I am taking a course in English at YMCA.

I am taking courses at the university.

résumé [rézumèi/rèzjuméi] 履歴書のことは、正式にはラテン語の curriculum vitae を使うが、普通には、フランス語から来た résumé を使う。なお、レジュメは論文などの「要約、まとめ」の意味でも使われる。

Point 3

Manager:	**May I look at them?**
Toshio:	**I hope they are all right. I wrote them in a hurry this morning.**
Manager:	**What sort of work did you do in this construction office?**
Toshio:	**I was in charge of books in the business department.**
Manager:	**I see. And you quit that job this June, right?**
Toshio:	**Yes, because, for one thing, I wanted to study English, and find a job where English is really needed.**

in a hurry「大急ぎで」

I was in a hurry to catch the train.

I was in charge of ...「私は…の責任者でした」ただの係員、事務員のときは in charge of と言ってはいけない。

She is in charge of our class.（クラス担任）

I am working in the sales department.（営業部員）

I see.「なるほど」相づちの言葉。

quit that job「その仕事を辞めた」quit は無変化の動詞で、反対に「仕事につく」なら、take a job。

I want to quit my job and take a better one.

this June 今が７月以降であるときの「今年の６月」。今が５月以前であれば、「去年の６月」となるから last June と言う。

right? いま言ったことに念を押す言い方。

You broke this, right? / He did it, right?

for one thing「一つには」

For one thing I like this job.

Point 4

Manager:	**Well, in that case, our export business here will give you all the chance you need to practice English.**
Toshio:	**Will you give me a chance?**
Manager:	**I don't see why not. When can you start?**
Toshio:	**Anytime you say, sir.**
Manager:	**Then report here at eight tomorrow morning.**
Toshio:	**Eight in the morning. Thank you, sir.**
Manager:	**Glad you came in.**

in that case「もしそうなら」

In that case I won't take the job.

In that case I'll find a job in my home town.

give me a chance「機会を与える」これは機会を与えて（雇って）頑張ってもらうという意味でよく使う。

He gave me a chance and I did my best.

I don't see why not.「いけないわけはない。もちろんいいでしょう。」これは「よろしいいとも」という気持ちを伝える決まり文句。

Anytime you say.「いつでも」

Anytime you say will be OK with me.

report here「出頭してください」report は「報告する」の意味ではなく、出てきて仕事を始める準備ができたことを知らせるという意味で使う畏まった言葉。

What time do you have to report?

「出勤は何時ですか」

Glad you came in. これは自分を訪ねてくれた人が去るときの挨拶の言葉。

実力チェック　**英語で言ってみよう！**

1. あなたはこれを壊（こわ）したのね。
2. あなたは今どんなお仕事をしていますか。
3. もちろん、いいですよ。
4. それなら別の仕事を探します。
5. 私はいつでも結構（けっこう）です。
6. 私は金曜の 9 時にブラウン教授の研究室 (Professor Brown's office) に出向いた。

Dialog Sixteen

ENJOYING THE EVENING COOL

夕涼み

これは昭和21年8月、戦争が終ってからちょうど1年後に放送されたものである。風呂に入って洗いたてのゆかたを着、下駄履き(げたば)で庭に出て天の川(あまのがわ)を見上げる。まだ戦災復興の工場からの煙が夜空を曇(くも)らせることもないきれいな空だったことであろう。弟のことをてきぱきと世話するこの姉のような気立ての女性は、日本人がいつまでも失いたくない宝である。

Enjoying the Evening Cool

Mari: **How was the bath, Taro?**

Taro : **Boy! I feel good.**

Mari: **Well, put on your *yukata*.**

Taro: **Do I have a clean one, Mari?**

Mari: **Yes, it's by the bureau there.**

Taro: **Oh, great! Thanks.**

Mari: **Now, when you're ready, come out to the garden.**

Taro: **Just a minute. I have to dry off.**

Mari: **Don't leave the towel on the floor.**

Taro: **OK, OK. I'll hang it up here.**

Mari: **Hurry! Come on out, Taro. It's really nice.**

Taro: **I'm coming. Here, Mari. I've got a fan for you.**

Mari: **Good. I was just going to tell you to bring one.**

Taro: **It's cool out here, isn't it?**

Mari : **Yes. And look at the stars. Aren't they pretty?**

Taro: **You're right! They are so bright and clear I can almost count them.**

Mari: **These darn mosquitoes!**

Taro: **What are those white things stretching across the sky? Are they clouds?**

Mari: **No, that's the Milky Way.**

Taro: **Really? I thought they were just clouds.**

Mari : **Hey! Look at those big stars over there.**

Taro: **So what do you call them?**

Mari: **Those seven big stars are called the Big Dipper.**

Taro: **The Big Dipper? Why?**

Mari: **Because they look like a dipper, I guess.**

真理　お風呂はどうだった。

太郎　ああ、いい気持ち。

真理　さあ、ゆかたを着て。

太郎　洗濯(せんたく)したのがあるの、お姉ちゃん。

真理　ええ、たんすのそばにおいてあるわよ。

太郎　わあ、うれしい、ありがとう。

真理　用意ができたら、お庭へいらっしゃいよ。

太郎　ちょっと待って、まだよく拭(ふ)かなくちゃ。

真理　すんだらタオルを下に置かないでね。

太郎　うん、いいよ。ここにかけとく。

真理　早くね。さあ出ていらっしゃい。とてもいいわよ。

太郎　すぐ行く。はい、お姉ちゃん、うちわ持ってきたよ。

真理　あら、いま持ってきてと言おうと思っていたところよ。

太郎　ここは涼(すず)しいね。

真理　ええ、それに空を見てごらん、きれいでしょう。

太郎　うん、よく光ってるね、はっきりと。まるで数えられるようだ。

真理　いやね、この蚊(か)。

太郎　あの空に広がった白いものは何だろう。雲かな。

真理　違うわ。あれは天の川よ。

太郎　そう言うの、あれ。ぼくはまた雲かと思った。

真理　ほら、あちらの大きな星を見てごらん。

太郎　うん、あれは何って言うの。

真理　あの七つの大きな星ね。あれは北斗七星(ひしゃく)って言うのよ。

太郎　ひしゃくだって。どうして。

真理　きっと、ひしゃくの形をしているからでしょう。

Taro: **You mean those four in a square and three of them coming out this way like the handle?**
Mari: **That's the idea.**

Point 1

Mari: **How was the bath, Taro?**
Taro : **Boy! I feel good.**
Mari: **Well, put on your *yukata*.**
Taro: **Do I have a clean one, Mari?**
Mari: **Yes, it's by the bureau there.**
Taro: **Oh, great! Thanks.**
Mari: **Now, when you're ready, come out to the garden.**

How was ...?「どうだったの。」

How was the concert? — Boy, it was really good.
How was the food? — Well, it was all right.
How was the sale? — Boy, it was crowded.

I feel good.「いい気持ちです。」

I feel fine.「けっこうです。」
I feel at home.「気楽です、くつろぎます。」
I feel bad.「気分が悪い。」

put on「着る、かぶる、はく」反対は put off.

Put on your shoes and go outside.
Put on your jeans and wash the dishes.

Do I have ...?「…はありますか」大変便利な言い方。

Do we have enough gas? / Do we have apples for dessert?
「ガソリンは大丈夫かしら。」

clean「汚れていない、洗濯してある」反対は used.

Clean towels are by the mirror.
Put the used towels in this basket.

太郎　ああ、あの四つが四角(しかく)になって、こちらに出てる三つが柄(え)になっているわけだね。

真理　そうよ。

Point 2

Taro: **Just a minute. I have to dry off.**
Mari: **Don't leave the towel on the floor.**
Taro: **OK, OK. I'll hang it up here.**
Mari: **Hurry! Come on out, Taro. It's really nice.**
Taro: **I'm coming. Here, Mari. I've got a fan for you.**
Mari: **Good. I was just going to tell you to bring one.**

I'll have to ... first「先ず…しなければならない」

I'll have to feed the dog first.

I'll have to speak to Mom first.

leave「置いておく」won't は will not の略。

Don't leave meat on the table. — OK, I won't.

Don't leave the food in the car. — OK, I won't.

up here「ここに」これは here だけでもよいが、会話のときはこの up をよく使う。ただし、up には別に意味はない。

The bus stop is up there.「バス停はあそこです。」

The subway station is up there.

Mari 日本語では「お姉さん」だが、英語では必ず名前を言う。

I've got = I have got = I have. 最重要の言い方。

for you は「してあげる」といった感じのときに使う。

I've got good news for you. — What is it?

I've got something nice for you. — Oh, great!

I was just going to ...「ちょうど…しようとしていた」

I was just going to do it myself.

I was just going to tell you about her.

Point 3

Taro: **It's cool out here, isn't it?**
Mari: **Yes. And look at the stars. Aren't they pretty?**
Taro: **You're right! They are so bright and clear I can almost count them.**
Mari: **These darn mosquitoes!**
Taro: **What are those white things stretching across the sky? Are they clouds?**
Mari: **No, that's the Milky Way.**
Taro: **Really? I thought they were just clouds.**

It's ..., isn't it?「…ですね」同意を求めるときに使う。

It's hot in here, isn't it? / Your car is beautiful, isn't it?

Aren't they pretty?「きれいね。」質問ではなく感嘆している言い方だから、最後の語を上げて下げる。

Look at those rabbits. Aren't they lovely?

Look at the baby. Isn't she beautiful?

so bright and clear (that) ...「あまり…なので…」この that は会話ではよく省略される。

The suit is so expensive (that) I can't buy it.

almost「もう少しで、ほとんど」

It was so moving I almost cried.

「感動的で泣きそうになった。」

It was so nice that I almost got it.

darn「いまいましい、ちくしょう」など強い不快感を表す。

I thought they were just clouds.「ただの雲と思った。」

I thought they were just sparrows.「すずめ」

I thought he was just a stranger.「よその人」

Point 4

Mari: **Hey! Look at those big stars over there.**
Taro: **So what do you call them?**
Mari: **Those seven big stars are called the Big Dipper.**
Taro: **The Big Dipper? Why?**
Mari: **Because they look like a dipper, I guess.**
Taro: **You mean those four in a square and three of them coming out this way like the handle?**
Mari: **That's the idea.**

What do you call ...?「…は何と言いいますか。」人に尋ねるときに、この言葉を覚えておくと便利である。

What do you call those trains?
— They are called "shinkansen" or bullet trains.

What do you call that? — It's called Tokyo Tower.

look like「のようだ。に似ている」

They look like each other.「よく似ているね。」

They look like twins.「ふたごのようだ。」

I guess.「だろうと思う。」推量で言うときに使う。文の前でも後でも良い。

Mom went shopping, I guess.

I guess he is from America.

You mean ...?「…ですか」確かめるとき使う。

Dad is in Kyoto now.「父さんはいま京都よ。」
— You mean he is not coming home?「帰らないのね。」

That's the idea.「そのとおり。」これも決まった言い方。英語らしく聞こえるように言い方に注意。「そうそう、そのとおり」と感じを出して言えば良い。

実力チェック　　英語で言ってみよう！

1. コンサート (the concert) はどうでしたか。
2. ここに掛(か)けておくわね。
3. これは何と言うんですか。
4. 週刊誌 (weekly magazine) をもって来ましたよ。
5. あまりに可愛(かわい)いので買いそうになった。

カムカム英語と私たち

池見 清志

平川先生が与えて下さった英語との出会い

平川唯一先生の「カムカム英会話講座」が始まった1946年2月と言えば、太平洋戦争が終結して半年が経過し、戦時中は「敵国語」として使用も教育も固く禁じられていた英語も復活し、巷にはアメリカからの輸入文化と英語が溢（あふ）れ始めていた。

テレビはおろか民間放送も存在しなかった当時は、耳から入る情報源としてはNHKのラジオ放送しかなく、日本人の多くが「カムカム英語」に聞き入ったという。当時、小学校5年生から6年生になろうとしていた私もそのなかの一人で、毎日、夕方になるとラジオにかじりついて15分間の番組に耳を傾（かたむ）けた。

なぜ私が英語に興味を持ったのかは記憶にないが、この番組のお陰で英語が非常に好きになり、熱心に勉強するようになったのは事実だ。

時は流れて1968年4月のある日、私は本田技研で海外向けの広報や宣伝の仕事をしていたが、上司が私のところに来て、「平川唯一さんの娘さんがわが社に就職したいと言ってきているので、面接して英語の力を見てくれ」と言われた。

そこで初めて旧姓平川萬里子さんに会って話し合い、その結果を「人物、英語力ともに申し分なく、是非採用したい」と上司に報告した。彼女は私と同じ部署に配属になり、何年か楽しく一緒に仕事をするとともに、彼女を通じて平川先生にもお近づきする機会を得た。

1969年3月に私が最初の海外出張でカナダのトロントでひと月ほど仕事をし、羽田に帰国した時に、萬里子さんだけでなく、先生までが出迎えに来て下さったのには、びっくりするとともに恐縮(きょうしゅく)の至(いた)りだったのを覚えている。

萬里子さんは日本舞踊の道に専念するために1974年に本田技研を退社され、会社にとっても、私にとっても大きな損失となったが、その後の彼女が大成され、米国シアトルにKabuki Academyを創設して日本の伝統芸能の国際的な普及に活躍しておられるのを見れば、正しい選択をされたことが理解できる。

1993年8月に、私は出張先のロンドンで家内から電話を受け、先生が他界されたことを知った。ご葬儀に参列できなかったことは痛恨(つうこん)の極(きわ)みだったが、家内を出席させた。

私の生涯を振り返ると、18歳だった1953年に当時としては珍しく米国に6年間留学する機会を与えられた時から、その後の社会人としての人生、さらには定年退職後も英語とは切っても切れないものだった。本田技研在職中には、車の排気ガス削減技術の米国メーカーへのライセンス供与、米国での生産工場建設のための土地選定、英国自動車メーカーとの提携(ていけい)等のプロジェクトで海外の企業や政府機関との交渉に参加し、マスキー法に関する米国議会の公聴会での証言もした。本田宗一郎氏が米国のミシガン工科大学から名誉博士号を授与された時の記念講演の原稿を草案したり、英国のダイアナ妃殿下(ひでんか)が狭山工場を見学された際にはご案内兼ご説明係という大役を務めたことも忘れ難い思い出である。こうした活動の基礎となった英語との「出会い」を作って下さった平川先生には、八十路半ばを過ぎた現在でも感謝の念で一杯だ。

最期に、本書にこの文を寄稿する機会を与えて下さった萬里子さん、兄の平川洌さん、それに出版社の南雲堂にお礼を申し上げたい。

（いけみ・きよし／元本田技研工業株式会社参事）

Dialog Seventeen

A BICYCLE RIDE

サイクリング

これは平川英語には珍しくよその人との会話である。この自転車に乗った人は65歳になっている。この会話を書いた放送時の平川講師は40代の半ばであった。あのころは20年後は相当な老人と感じられたのであろう。その後、長寿社会になって、65歳は老人というには早すぎるが、孫がいる年齢だから「おじいさん」であることに違いはない。

A Bicycle Ride

Track-18

Taro: Ting-a-ing, ting-a-ing, ting-a-ing.

Yasui: Oh, cut it out! I heard you.

Taro: Hello, Mr. Yasui.

Yasui: Oh, hello, Taro. I didn't know it was you.

Taro: That's all right. But where are you going?

Yasui: No place in particular. I'm just taking a walk.

Taro: Taking a walk on a bicycle?

Yasui: Sure, there's nothing like it. I used to be a pretty good cyclist, you know.

Taro: No wonder I had a hard time catching up with you.

Yasui: Still, old age is creeping on. I'm sixty-five, you know.

Taro: But you still have the heart of a young man.

Yasui: I guess you're right at that.

Taro: Do you think you can make it up this hill?

Yasui: Don't worry. You just follow me, and see what I can do.

Taro: Are you sure?

Yasui: It's kind of hard at first, but I'll get used to it.

Taro: Do you think so?

Yasui: You'll see. I'm feeling easier already.

Taro: One, two, and one more push.

Yasui: There, my boy. We've made it.

Taro: Shall we get off and rest?

Yasui: Good idea. My heart is young, but not my feet.

Taro: My arm is tired.

Yasui: Your arm? How come?

Taro: Well, because I'm not used to pushing another bicycle, I guess.

太郎　チリンチリン、チリンチリン、チリンチリン。

安井　うるさいなあ、聞こえたよ。

太郎　おじいさん、こんにちは。

安井　やあ、太郎君か。いや、知らなかったもんで。

太郎　なあに、いいんですよ。おじいさんはどちらへ。

安井　別にどこということもない。ただの散歩(さんぽ)さ。

太郎　散歩ですか、自転車で。

安井　そう、いいもんだよ。これでも若い頃は相当(そうとう)な自転車乗りだったからね。

太郎　それでなかなか追(お)い付(い)けないと思った。

安井　いや、やっぱり年は年だね、もう 65 だからな。

太郎　でもお気持は若いものと変らないですね。

安井　うん、それはそうかもしれん。

太郎　どうです。この坂は登れますか。

安井　心配要(い)らんよ。ついてきてごらん。わしにやれるかどうか。

太郎　大丈夫ですか。

安井　初めはちょっと大変だが、すぐ慣(な)れるから。

太郎　そうかなあ。

安井　まあ、見ていなさい。さあ、もう楽になってきた。

太郎　一つに二つ、もう一押しと。

安井　さあよし。とうとう登ったぞ。

太郎　ちょっと降(お)りて休みましょうか。

安井　うんそれがいい。気持ちは若いが脚(あし)の方がだめだ。

太郎　ぼくは腕(うで)が疲(つか)れた。

安井　なに腕が。なんで。

太郎　ほかの自転車を押すのはどうも慣れないものですから。

A Bicycle Ride

Point 1

Taro: **Ting-a-ing, ting-a-ing, ting-a-ing.**
Yasui: **Oh, cut it out! I heard you.**
Taro: **Hello, Mr. Yasui.**
Yasui: **Oh, hello, Taro. I didn't know it was you.**
Taro: **That's all right. But where are you going?**
Yasui: **No place in particular. I'm just taking a walk.**

Cut it out!「やめなさい。よせ。」Stop it! と同じ意味の俗語。

I heard you.「聞こえた。もう分かったよ。」安井のおじいさんが、こんな口のききかたをするのは、後から自転車で追いかけてくるのが自分の孫だとばかり思っているからである。

That's all right.「いいですよ。かまいませんよ。」I didn't know ... と組み合わせて練習しよう。

I din't know you did it. — That's all right.
I didn't know you were here. — That's all right.
I didn't know I was late. — That's all right.

No place in particular.「特にどこでもない。別にあてはない。」これは前に I have を省いた言い方である。

Nothing in particular.「別に何ということもない。」
Nobody in particular.「特に誰というわけでもない。」
No school in particular.
「別にどこの学校と決まっているわけではない。」

just taking a walk「散歩しているだけ」

I was just taking a rest.（休憩）
I was just taking a nap.（昼寝）

Point 2

Taro: **Taking a walk on a bicycle?**
Yasui: **Sure, there's nothing like it. I used to be a pretty good cyclist, you know.**
Taro: **No wonder I had a hard time catching up with you.**
Yasui: **Still, old age is creeping on. I'm sixty-five, you know.**
Taro: **But you still have the heart of a young man.**
Yasui: **I guess you're right at that.**

on a bicycle「自転車で」

I go to school on foot.（徒歩通学）

I go to work by bus.（バス通勤）

There's nothing like it.「こんないいものはない。」

I used to be a pretty good ...「以前はかなりの…だった」

I used to be a pretty good tennis player.

No wonder ...「だから…だ」

I had a hard time ...ing「…するのが大変だった」a hard time の後は必ず動詞の進行形 (ing のついた形) を使う。

No wonder I had a hard time finding the way.

..., you know 文末につけて、「…だからね」と念を押す言い方。

I got up early, you know. / I was very sleepy, you know.

Still, ...「それでも…」still が文中に来れば、「まだ…」

Still, you eat everything. / I still have the doll you gave me.

creeping on「しのび寄っている」

I guess inflation is creeping on.

you're right at that「そういえば君は正しい。君の言う通り」at that はなくても差し支えないが、会話に味をつける言葉。

I guess she is right at that.

Point 3

Taro: **Do you think you can make it up this hill?**
Yasui: **Don't worry. You just follow me, and see what I can do.**
Taro: **Are you sure?**
Yasui: **It's kind of hard at first, but I'll get used to it.**
Taro: **Do you think so?**
Yasui: **You'll see. I'm feeling easier already.**

make it up this hill「この坂を登る」make it は succeed の意味でいろいろな場合に使われる。はしごをかけるときでも、問題を解決するときでも、Can you make it? と言えばよい。また、come 又は arrive in time（間に合う）の意味でも使われる。

I tried it again and I made it.「再挑戦して成功した。」
I can't make it down this slope.「この傾斜地は下れない。」
I couldn't make it for the last bus.「終バスに間に合わなかった。」

see what I can do「私に何ができるか見ていなさい。まあ、見ていてごらん」

Are you sure?「確かですか。大丈夫ですか。」

kind of「ちょっと 」これは somewhat の意味の口語表現で、会話ではよく使われる。

I felt kind of sorry for him.
It was a kind of funny story.

get used to ...「…に慣れてくる、…が楽になる」
You'll soon get used to the weather.

You'll see.「今に分かるよ。」決まり文句。

I'm feeling easier already.「もう楽になってきた。」
I'm feeling better already.

Point 4

Taro: **One, two, and one more push.**
Yasui: **There, my boy. We've made it.**
Taro: **Shall we get off and rest?**
Yasui: **Good idea. My heart is young, but not my feet.**
Taro: **My arm is tired.**
Yasui: **Your arm? How come?**
Taro: **Well, because I'm not used to pushing another bicycle, I guess.**

There, my boy.「ほら、ね、君。」この my boy は年下の男の子に向かって言う言葉。女の子に言うときは、There. だけで、my girl はつけない。

We've made it.「とうとう出来た。やっとできた。」これは決まり文句だから、しっかり覚えよう。

get off「降りる」反対は get on。
Get off the bus at the third stop.「３番目の停留所で降りなさい。」

My arm is tired.「腕が疲れた。」ここで arm と単数になっているのは、片手は自分のハンドルを握り、もう一方が安井さんの自転車の後の荷台を押していたために疲れたからである。英語は両腕なら arms と複数形を使う。hand と hands も同じ。ビートルズが "I want to hold your hand" と歌うとき、彼は彼女の片手を握りたいと言っているのであって、「両手で抱きしめたい」と言っているのではない。

How come?「どう して。」Why? と同じ意味の俗語。
How come you are so late?

not used to pushing「押すのに慣れていない」to の後には動名詞が来る。
I'm not used to sitting up late.（夜更かし）
This dog is used to people.

実力チェック　英語で言ってみよう！

1. なんだ、君か。君だとは知らなかったよ。
2. こんないいものはない。
3. どうしてまた君は遅れたの。
4. 日本は苦労して世界の経済に追い付いた。
5. それもそうかもしれないね。
6. 彼女は遂(つい)にオペラ歌手になった。

Dialog Eighteen

A GOOD SKIER

スキーの名手

ここにも英語会話に役立つ言い方がいっぱいある。姉がまだ数日はかかるというセーターを太郎はうまい具合(ぐあい)に話して明日中に仕上(しあ)げてもらうことに成功するが、その心理作戦がこの話のポイントであろう。考えて見れば、このようなことはわれわれの身近(みぢか)でもときどき起(お)こる。この会話には、語法的に日本人が最(もっと)も不得意とする by と until の使い分けなども出て来る。

A Good Skier

Track-19

Taro: **How are you coming on with my sweater, Mari?**

Mari: **Oh, just a few more days, and it'll all he finished.**

Taro: **Will it take that long?**

Mari: **I believe so. I still have both sleeves to knit.**

Taro: **Can't you finish it by tomorrow night?**

Mari: **No, because I have to do a lot of other stuff, too.**

Taro: **Oh, I can do all that if you will work on my sweater.**

Mari: **That'll be a big help, but why do you want it in such a hurry?**

Taro: **Because I've been talking to Mom.**

Mari: **Well, what about?**

Taro: **I told her how good you were at both skiing and knitting.**

Mari: **But she's never seen me ski.**

Taro: **I know. That's why she said that you may be a good skier, but ....**

Mari: **But I am a very slow knitter, is that it?**

Taro: **That's it. So I said Mari could finish my sweater by tomorrow night.**

Mari: **Then what did Mom say?**

Taro: **She said if you could, she would let you and me go on a skiing trip the day after.**

Mari: **Did she really?**

Taro: **Yes, but I didn't know you had so much left to do.**

Mari: **Don't worry. You'll be skiing on Sunday.**

Dialog Eighteen

A Good Skier

太郎　姉さん、ぼくのセーターどう。もうだいぶ出来たの。

真埋　そう、もうあと二三日で出来上がりよ。

太郎　まだそんなにかかるの。

真理　多分ね。まだこれからそでを両方編むんだから。

太郎　あしたの晩までに出来ないかなあ。

真理　無理よ、だってほかのこともしなくっちゃならないんだから。

太郎　なんだ、それならぼくみんなやるよ、姉さんがセーターをやってくれるなら。

真理　それだったら助かるけど、でもなんでそんなに急いでこれがいるの。

太郎　だって、ぼくお母さんと話していたんだ。

真理　あら、なんのことを。

太郎　ぼくね、姉さんはスキーも編み物もとても上手だって言ったの。

真理　だってお母さんは、まだ私のスキー見たことないわ。

太郎　うん、それでね、姉さんはスキーの方はうまいかしれないけれど…

真理　だけど、編み物はのろいっていうんでしょう。

太郎　そう。だから、姉さんはぼくのセーターを明日の晩までにはきっと仕上げるよって言ったの。

真理　そしたらお母さんはなんて？

太郎　お母さんはね、もしそれが出来たら、姉さんもぼくもあさってスキーに行っていいって。

真理　あら、ほんと？

太郎　うん、でもまだそんなにかかるって、ぼく知らなかったからね。

真理　大丈夫よ。日曜日にはきっとスキーができるようにしてあげるわ。

A Good Skier

Point 1

Taro: **How are you coming on with my sweater, Mari?**
Mari: **Oh, just a few more days, and it'll all he finished.**
Taro: **Will it take that long?**
Mari: **I believe so. I still have both sleeves to knit.**
Taro: **Can't you finish it by tomorrow night?**
Mari: **No, because I have to do a lot of other stuff, too.**

How are you coming on with ...?「…の進み具合はどうですか。…はもうだいぶできましたか。」with ... に注意。

Mari 日本語では「お姉さん」のように言うが、英語では名前を呼ぶ。兄弟姉妹は互いに名前で呼ぶ。

just a few more days, and ...「あと何日かすれば…」時間を示す語だけで「たったら」という感じを表している。

Just three more days, and we'll be out of school.

「あと３日で休みだ。」

Just one more year, and you'll graduate.

「あと１年で卒業だね。」

that long「そんなに長く」この that は「そんなに」という意味の副詞。this も that も副詞的によく使われる。

Will it cost that much?

Will it take that long?

My cat is this big.「私の猫はこれくらいです。」

have both sleeves to knit「両袖を編まね ばならない」have ... to ... は「…を…しなければならない」。

I have much work to do today.

I have two cats to feed.

by tomorrow night「明日の夜までに」by を until と混同しないこと。until は継続して「…まで」。

I can't finish it by noon. Can you wait until 3:00?

Point 2

Taro: **Oh, I can do all that if you will work on my sweater.**
Mari: **That'll be a big help, but why do you want it in such a hurry?**
Taro: **Because I've been talking to Mom.**
Mari: **Well, what about?**
Taro: **I told her how good you were at both skiing and knitting.**

if you will work on ... 条件節だから if you work on ... でいいはずだが、「やってくれるなら」という感じのときは、will を付けてもよい。work の次には on を使うことに注意。

What are you working on now?

I am working on the housing project now.
「いま住宅計画をやっています。」

I am on the project team.

That'll be a big help.「それは大助かりだ。」次のように言われたとき、この決まり文句で答えてみよう。

I can baby-sit for you.「子守はしますよ。」

I can cook tonight.「今夜は私が料理してもいいよ。」

in such a hurry「そんなに急いで」

Why are you in such a hurry?

Where was he going in such a hurry?

good at ...「…が上手」

I am good at making *onigiri*.

I am not good at mathematics.「数学は苦手だ。」

both ... and ...「…も…も」

I like both coffee and tea.

I am good at both basketball and tennis.

Point 3

Mari: **But she's never seen me ski.**

Taro: **I know. That's why she said that you may be a good skier, but ....**

Mari: **But I am a very slow knitter, is that it?**

Taro: **That's it. So I said Mari could finish my sweater by tomorrow night.**

she's never seen me ski「私がスキーをするのを見たことがない」

I've never seen him run.

I've never seen him walk past our house.「家のそばを通り過ぎる」

That's why ...「だから…」

That's why she could't come today.

That's why I said she could't come today.

That's why I like this book.

slow knitter「縫うのが遅い」反対は fast knitter。

He is a slow learner, but a good writer.

「彼は覚えが悪いが、文章はうまい。」

may be a good ..., but ...「…は上手かもしれないが…」

I may be a good swimmer, but not a good singer.

「泳ぎは上手かもしれないけど、歌は下手です。」

I may be a slow learner, but a hard worker.

..., is that it?「…でしょう」念を押すときに付けて言う決まり文句。これに対して「そうだ」のときは That's right. で良い。

You were not there, is that right? — That's right.

「現場にはいなかったのか。」　「そうです。」

He did this, is that right? — That's right.

by tomorrow night「あすの夜までに」

Can you finish it by tomorrow noon?

Can you finish it by the day after?

Point 4

Mari: **Then what did Mom say?**
Taro: **She said if you could, she would let you and me go on a skiing trip the day after.**
Mari: **Did she really?**
Taro: **Yes, but I didn't know you had so much left to do.**
Mari: **Don't worry. You'll be skiing on Sunday.**

go on a skiing trip「スキーに行く」

We went on a hiking trip last Sunday.

I want to go on a golfing trip soon.

the day after「明後日」

It will be finished the day after.

It will be finished by the day after.

had so much left to do「仕上げるまでにはまだそんなにあるとは」

I have fifty more pages left to read.

「後５０ページ残っている」

I have so little left to do.

「後はもう少ししか残っていない」

You'll be skiing on Sunday.「日曜日にはスキーができますよ。」ここは「あなたにスキーができるようにしてあげます」という意味で、昔は文法的には You shall ... と言ったものだが、いまは単純未来 will を使う。

Don't worry. You'll be seeing her the day after.

Don't worry. You'll be in Tokyo this weekend.

Don't worry. You'll soon be going to America.

実力チェック　英語で言ってみよう！

1. あなたのレポート (paper) のでき具合(ぐあい)はいかがですか。
2. あと 2 週間もすればでき上(あ)がると思います。
3. 4 時までに私の家へ来られますか。
4. そんなに急(いそ)いでどこへ行ってたの。
5. 彼がそんな金持ちなんて知らなかったな。
6. 彼が勉強している姿は見たことがない 。

カムカム英語と私たち

カムカムおじさんとわたしのカナダ生活

パーカー 敬子

終戦後 2, 3 年目のある日、中学生の私は駅前の露店本屋でカムカム英語のテキストを買った。毎晩の NHK の放送が楽しみだった。先生は自分で文を音読された後、沈黙、その時私は発音を真似る。すると先生は “That's it!” と褒めて下さる。この番組には講師と生徒の間に目に見えない繋がりがあった。先生に手紙を書いたら、私の家の近所に Go Go 支部があると教えていただき入会し、金曜日には支部の会にも参加して英語力は向上した。

高校 2 年生のとき、私はペンパルズクラブの部長として世界中のペンパルと文通していた。後に夫となるカナダ人の John Parker から手紙が届き、大学を卒業するまでの 6 年間、彼と文通を続けた。私の専攻は英文学だったので、英系カナダ人の彼とは話が合った。

大学卒業後、私はカナダ（Vancouver）に渡り、彼と結婚した。最初の 1 年間は、主婦業のほか、小、中、高の非常勤教諭、2 年目からは高校の常勤教諭として英語、数学、カナダ史などを教え、その後、我が家の教室で始めた音楽理論の授業は 46 年間続いた。2016 年には、トロント王立音楽院から第 1 回の Teacher of Distinction 賞を受賞する栄誉に浴した。家庭では二男一女に恵まれ、息子たちは二人とも NewYork の Juilliard 音楽院を卒業、同院で博士号を取得し、現在でもカナダを代表する二人のコンサートピアニストとして世界で活躍する一方、大学の教授として後進の育成に励んでいる。娘はバンクーバー響、カナダ国営放送局、トロント響などを経て、今はフリーランスとして音楽分野で仕事をしている。

私自身は46年の音楽理論とピアノ教師を引退後、1998年から在Vancouver近郊の日本人女性を対象の“音楽の会”と、カナダ人も含めた“Jane Austen (英国小説家) を英語で読む会”を現在まで23年間自宅で主催(しゅさい)している。また桜楓会（楓はカナダのシンボルで、カナダに永住している日系シニアの会）の会員であり、Jane Austen Society of North AmericaのVancouver支部の幹部の一人として活動している。

日本の文化（茶道、華道など）と音楽理論、ピアノ実技、そしてそれらに関わる英語の全部を知っている人が少ないので、いろいろな団体、イベントなどで通訳を頼まれたり、老人ホームや学校などから講演、実演などを依頼されることも多く、可能な限り日加友好のために受けることにしている。

思い起こせば、大昔に平川先生から誰にでも英語で話しかける友好的な態度と自信を持たせていただいたことが私の人生の始まりでした。今後も日加友好のために微力(びりょく)を尽(つ)くしたいと思います。

（パーカー・けいこ／北米ジェーン・オースチン協会（JASNA）バンクーバー支部長、同協会エッセイコンクール審査員）

Dialog Nineteen

REALLY SIMILAR BUT DIFFERENT
似ているようで違う

母と子が父の帰りを待つ。足音を聞きつけて「あ、お父さんだ」とみんなで玄関に出迎えに行く。これは昔から日本の暮らしの一部であった。最近は、子供が大きくなると父親の権威もなくなる傾向が強いが、この会話には父親健在の時代を思い浮かべさせるものがある。私自身、子供たちがまだ小学生のころ、昭和50年代のことだったと思うが、NHKの大河ドラマで、主人公の侍が帰宅すると家族が玄関口に跪き、深々と頭を下げて出迎えるというのがあった。わが家ではこれを真似て、家族が廊下に座って両手をつき「父上、お帰りなされませ」と私を出迎えてくれた年があった。みんなも小さいころ「あっ、パパだ」と出迎えていたころを思い出しながら、やってみよう。

Really Similar but Different

Track-20

Taro: The dog is barking. Maybe Dad's home.

Mom: I don't think so. He said he would be late tonight.

Taro: Then it's Uncle Akio, maybe. No, it isn't, either.

Mom: No? Why do you say that?

Taro: I can tell if it's Uncle Akio.

Mom: By his footsteps, you mean?

Taro: No, by his "Ahem."

Mom: Oh, the way he clears his throat.

Taro: That's right. He always does that when he is near the house.

Mom: For that matter, Dad has the same habit, too.

Taro: I know. That's because they are brothers.

Mom: Their voices are really similar, too, aren't they?

Taro: That's what I say. They are almost like the twins.

Mom: They sure have a lot in common.

Taro: But I know one thing they don't.

Mom: Do you mean Uncle Akio's mustache?

Taro: No, not that. I massaged Uncle Akio's shoulder the other day.

Mom: That was nice of you. And what did he say?

Taro: He said, "Oh, I feel so much better!" But Dad is different.

Mom: Is he? How?

Taro: He just says nothing, and goes right to sleep.

太郎　あ、犬が鳴(な)いている。お父さんかな。

母　違うでしょう。今日は遅くなるってことだったから。

太郎　じゃ叔父(おじ)さんかな。いや、違う、違う。

母　あらそう？　なんで？

太郎　叔父さんだったら、ぼくすぐわかるもの。

母　足音でわかるの？

太郎　違う、エヘンって言うの。

母　ああ、咳払(せきばら)いのことね。

太郎　そう。家のそばへ来たら、きっとするんだもの。

母　そう言えばお父さんだって、同じような癖(くせ)があってよ。

太郎　そりゃ、だって兄弟なんだもの。

母　声だってそっくりなんだからね。

太郎　そう、本当だ。まるで双子みたいね。

母　よくあんなにも似(に)るものと思うくらい。

太郎　だけど一つだけ似ていない所があるよ。

母　それ、口ひげのこと？

太郎　違うよ。こないだ叔父さんの肩をもんであげたの。

母　あら、えらい。そしたらなんて言われたの。

太郎　そうしたら、「ああ、楽になったよ」って言ったの。でもお父さんは違うよ。

母　あらそう。どうして。

太郎　お父さんたら、なんにも言わないで、だまって眠りこむんだもの。

Point 1

Taro:	**The dog is barking. Maybe Dad's home.**
Mom:	**I don't think so. He said he would be late tonight.**
Taro:	**Then it's Uncle Akio, maybe. No, it isn't, either.**
Mom:	**No? Why do you say that?**
Taro:	**I can tell if it's Uncle Akio.**

barking「ほえている」動物の種類によって「鳴く」という動詞が違う。犬は bark、猫は meow、雄鶏は crow、鳥は sing または chirp などとそれぞれ異なることに注意。

Maybe Dad's home.「お父さんのお帰りかもしれない。」

I don't think so.「そうは思わない。」これは I think so. の否定形であるが、英語では「いいえ」という意味で大変よく使う言い方だから、しっかり覚えよう。

Do you want to go shopping? — I don't think so.
Are you planning to go abroad? — I don't think so.
Will you come with me? — I don't think so.

He said he would be home late tonight.「今夜は帰りが遅くなると言った。」He said と過去形の後では will be も過去形で would be となる。次の文を He said he would ... に変えて言ってみよう 。

"I'll be home as usual tonight".（いつもの 通り）
"I'll be out of town tomorrow".（明日は出張）
"I'll have a conference in Tokyo".（東京で会議）

I can tell「私には分かる」この tell は「言う」ではなく「分かる」の意味でよく使う。

I can tell what you are thinking about.
「何を考えているか分かる。」
I can't tell the difference between the two.
「二つの違いが分からない。」

Point 2

Mom: **By his footsteps, you mean?**
Taro: **No, by his "Ahem."**
Mom: **Oh, the way he clears his throat.**
Taro: **That's right. He always does that when he is near the house.**
Mom: **For that matter, Dad has the same habit, too.**
Taro: **I know. That's because they are brothers.**

By his footsteps「足音で」

I can tell her by her voice. / I can tell her by the way she talks.

He always does that.「彼がいつもそうする」always の置き場所を間違えないこと。

He always comes to school early.

He always says something funny in class.

for that matter「その点では、そう言えば」

For that matter, I am a sumo fan myself.

For that matter, Japan is importing a lot.

the same habit「同じくせ」same にはいつも定冠詞 the がつく。habit は個人が習慣的にすることで（例えば、朝は６時に起きるとか、毎朝ジョギングをするとか）、これを custom（国民が習慣的に行うこと）と混同しないこと。

I have a habit of jogging before breakfast.
— Me, too. I have the same habit.

We always celebrate Christmas.
— We don't have that custom in Japan.

That's because ...「それは…だからだ」原因を表す。次の文を That's why ... として意味の違いを考えてみよう。

That's because you studied hard.

That's because we missed the train.

Point 3

Mom: **Their voices are really similar, too, aren't they?**
Taro: **That's what I say. They are almost like the twins.**
Mom: **They sure have a lot in common.**
Taro: **But I know one thing they don't.**
Mom: **Do you mean Uncle Akio's mustache?**

similar「よく似ている」これは different の反対。「…です ね」の言い方を練習しよう。

Your car and mine are very similar, aren't they?
Your teacher and ours are different, aren't they?

That's what I say.「そうだとも。その通り。」これは相づちの言葉であるから、気持ちを込めて That's を強く言う。That's exactly what I say. ともよく言う。

almost「ほとんど、もう少しで」次の文の違いを考えてみよう。

They are twins.
They are like the twins.
They are almost like the twins.

have lots of things in common「似たところがたくさんある。共通点が多い」

Chicago and Osaka have lots of things in common.

Do you mean?「…のことですか」これは聞き返すときの決まり文句だから、大変重宝である。mustache [mʌ́stæʃ] は「口ひげ」。なお、あごひげは beard、ほおひげは whisker。

Do you mean my twin brother?（ふたごの兄）
Do you mean his wife?
Do you mean the new mayor?（市長）

Point 4

Taro: **No, not that. I massaged Uncle Akio's shoulder the other day.**
Mom: **That was nice of you. And what did he say?**
Taro: **He said, "Oh, I feel so much better!" But Dad is different.**
Mom: **Is he? How?**
Taro: **He just says nothing, and goes right to sleep.**

No, not that. 「いや、そういうわけじゃない。それとは違う。」相づちの言葉。

No, not that. I was thinking of something else.（ほかのこと）
No, not that. I just want to sleep.

the other day 「このあいだ」

A strange thing happened to me the other day.
「このあいだ変なことが起きた。」
The other day I bought a new suit.

I feel so much better. 「私はずっといい気持ちになった。とても楽になった。」

I feel good. / I feel better.
I feel much better. / I feel so much better.

He just says nothing. これは He just doesn't say anything. と同じであるが、こちらのほうがよく使われる。

I just did nothing. / I just bought nothing.

goes right to sleep 「すぐ寝てしまう」right は日本語の「すぐ」に当たる。口調でつけるだけで、He just goes to sleep. と同じく、なくても意味に変りはない。

実力チェック　　**英語で言ってみよう！**

1. お母さんは朝のうちに買い物に行くと言っていた。
2. お父さんは歩き方（かた）で分かる。
3. 太郎はいつもそうだからね。
4. そう言えば、次郎にもそんな癖（くせ）がある。
5. それは二人がよく似ているからだよ。

平川唯一 (1902-1993)
あの世へグッバイしたカムカムおじさん

証城寺の狸ばやしの軽快なメロディに乗って、NHK ラジオで平川唯一氏の英会話講座が始まったのは昭和 21 年 2 月。その明るい声と会話に横溢するユーモアは、終戦直後の、混乱の中にも希望のある不思議に明るい気分にマッチして、たちまち高聴取率を獲得、「カムカムおじさん」と親しまれた。

彼の語学は、戦前 20 年間の滞米生活を通して身についたものである。岡山県の農家の次男として生れ、16 歳の時、アメリカへ出稼ぎに行った父親を迎えにワシントン州のシアトルへ行くが、そのまま父親と一緒に居ついてしまう。線路工夫や皿洗い、店番などをして働くが、「どんな苦労も、岡山での夜なべ仕事に比べれば楽しいものだった」と後年彼は述懐している。19 歳の時に小学校 1 年に入り直して英語を覚え、ハイスクールからワシントン州立大学へ入学。演劇を学び、卒業したら 30 歳になっていた。

不況の真っ只中で、ロサンゼルスでハリウッド映画の端役に出演したり、副牧師を務めたりするうち、女子留学生と知り合って結婚、現地の教会で挙式する。よね子夫人である。

昭和 12 年、生れたばかりの長男を抱いて帰国。NHK 海外放送要員に応募、国際部のチーフアナウンサーに就任した。日米開戦の特別放送を全世界に向けて行い、終戦時には昭和天皇の玉音放送を翻訳放送した。

だが彼はいったん NHK を辞職せざるを得なくなったことがある。GHQ が西新橋の NHK の施設をかなり乱暴なやり方で接収したが、その際に道案内したのが平川氏だったため、彼は占領軍の手先とみなされ、NHK 役員の怒りを買ったのである。

しかし、NHK に英会話の番組が設置されると平川氏が番組を担当することになった。カムカム英語の始まりである。「父は恥ずかしがり屋で、人と話すことは決して得意ではない。ラジオを聞いていると、スムースにアドリブを連発しているようですが、実際は事前に全部原稿に書き込んでいて、毎朝、テキストの前で、自ら笑いながら声を出し、リハーサルをやっていました。」(次男の平川クラレンス氏)

カムカム英語は昭和 26 年 3 月まで 5 年間続いた。この間に手元に来たファンレターは 50 万通を超えたという。民放が生まれると、そこへ場を移してさらに 5 年間。ラジオ放送のかたわら、世田谷の自宅でもカムカム英語センターを開設し、生きた英語を教えた。

平川氏はまた、外国映画の日本語吹き替えの先駆者でもある。テレビ映画の輸入会社太平洋テレビの副社長に就任し、「ララミー牧場」などを翻訳した。

晩年はもっぱら趣味のテニス三昧。伝統のある東京ローンテニスクラブのメンバーで、愛車の 1952 年型モーリスを運転して週に 4 日はクラブへ通った。85 歳までプレイを続けたという。皇太子、同妃殿下時代の天皇、皇后両陛下もテニス仲間で、美智子皇后は少女時代カムカム英語の熱心な生徒でもあったという。

転んで腰を痛め、8 月 25 日、91 年の生涯を閉じた。

(『週刊新潮』1993 年 9 月 9 日号「墓碑銘」から転載)

Dialog Twenty

WAITING FOR SPRING
春待ちて

ここで叔父さんはシェイクスピアを思わせる古風な文学的な言葉を使って話しかけている。普通に言っては照れ臭い内容なので、叔父さんは古風な言い方で照れ隠しをしているのである。シェイクスピアは秀吉と同じ時代の人だが、この４百年間、英語は基本的には変っていない。それでも現代英語と比べると言い方が古風であるから、特別な言い方をしていることはすぐに分かる。

Dialog Twenty

Waiting for Spring

Track-21

Uncle: **When winter comes, spring is not far off.**

Mari: **But, spring is here already, isn't it?**

Uncle: **I guess you're right. Spring! Oh, glorious spring!**

Mari: **Come on, Uncle Akio! What's the matter with you today?**

Uncle: **Know you my dream of dreams?**

Mari: **Nay, I know not .... Oh, nuts! What am I saying?**

Uncle: **Do you know the story called *Waiting for Spring*?**

Mari: **N ... no. Is it in English?**

Uncle: **In Japanese, of course. It's a great masterpiece.**

Mari: **Funny I've never heard of it. You don't mean *Spring*, do you?**

Uncle: **No, no. That's by Shimazaki Toson. I don't mean that one.**

Mari: **Is it better than that?**

Uncle: **M ... maybe.**

Mari: **Is it a sad story?**

Uncle: **Terribly sad, but it's romantic and thrilling.**

Mari: **I didn't know there was a story like that.**

Uncle: **There is. Do you want to read it?**

Mari: **Absolutely. Where is it?**

Uncle: **Well, it may come out in a month or so.**

Mari: **Then it's a new story. Who is it by?**

Uncle: **By Akio Aoki.**

Mari: **By you?**

Uncle: **Yes, I have entered a contest for the best novel.**

Dialog Twenty

Waiting for Spring

叔父　冬来(きた)りなば春遠からじ、か。

真理　あら、もう春じゃないの。

叔父　うん、もう春だ。春や春、と。

真理　いやだわ、叔父さん。どうしたの今日は。

叔父　君知るや、わが望み。

真理　いな、われ知らず。まあ、わたしまで変だわ。

叔父　『春待ちて』という小説知ってる？

真理　さあ。それ英語なの。

叔父　もちろん日本語さ。すごい傑作(けっさく)なんだ。

真理　変ねえ、聞いたことないけど。『春』っていうのと違うの？

叔父　いやいや。あれは島崎藤村のだろう。違うんだ。

真理　もっといいの？

叔父　かもしれない。

真理　泣かせるような話？

叔父　うん、とても。それにロマンチックでスリリングなんだ。

真理　そんなのあったかしら。

叔父　あるんだ。読みたいだろう。

真理　読みたいわ。どこにあるの。

叔父　さあ、もう一ヵ月くらいのうちに出るかもしれないけど。

真理　じゃあ新作なのね。誰の作？

叔父　青木明夫。

真理　まあ、叔父さんじゃないの。

叔父　うん、懸賞(けんしょう)小説に応募(おうぼ)したのさ。

Mari: **And you won?**

Uncle: **I hope so. That's what I'm waiting for.**

Point 1

Uncle: **When winter comes, spring is not far off.**
Mari: **But, spring is here already, isn't it?**
Uncle: **I guess you're right. Spring! Oh, glorious spring!**
Mari: **Come on, Uncle Akio! What's the matter with you today?**
Uncle: **Know you my dream of dreams?**
Mari: **Nay, I know not .... Oh, nuts! What am I saying?**

When spring comes, spring is not far off. これはイギリスの詩人シェレー (Percy Bysshe Shelley, 1792-1822) の詩 "Ode to the West Wind" の結びの文 "When Winter comes, can Spring be far behind?" を意識して言ったもの。これは「冬来たりなば春遠からじ」という訳で知られている。

Spring is here.「春が来た。もう春だ。」この here という語は「ここ」という意味だけでなく、いろいろ使い分けられる。

John is here already.「ジョンはもう来ました。」

Look here.「ああ、ちょっと。」

you're right.「その通り。」

Come on!「よしなさい。まあいやだ。」これは慣用語。言い方に注意。

What's the matter with you?「どうしたんですか。」

What's the matter with your car?

Know you ...? = Do you know ...? の古風な言い方。

my dream of dreams「私の最も切望するところ。最大の望み」

Nay, I know not. = No, I don't know. の古風な言い方。叔父さんの言い方にひかれて、思わず古風な言い方で答えたもの。

Oh, nuts.「まあ、いやだ。」軽蔑、失望を表す 感嘆詞。いつも s を付けて言う。

真理　それで当選したの？
叔父　それを願(わが)って待ってるんだよ。

Point 2

Uncle: **Do you know the story called *Waiting for Spring*?**
Mari: **N ... no. Is it in English?**
Uncle: **In Japanese, of course. It's a great masterpiece.**
Mari: **Funny I've never heard of it. You don't mean *Spring*, do you?**
Uncle: **No, no. That's by Shimazaki Toson. I don't mean that one.**

the story called ... 「…という小説」

Do you know the singer called Madonna?

Do you know the movie called "Rashomon"?

Do you know the restaurant called "Diana"?

in English? 「英語で」

He gave a lecture in English. / He spoke to us in Japanese.

I am writing an article in English.
「いま英語の論文を書いています。」

Funny I've never heard of it. 厳密には、It is funny that ... であるが、「変ねえ、私は聞いたことがないわ」といった感じで言う。

Funny I can't remember his name.

Funny you've never met her.

You don't mean ..., do you? 「…ではないんでしょうね。」次の問に「いや、それのことではない」と返事してください。

You don't mean *Bocchan* by Soseki, do you?

You don't mean Hepburn, do you?

Point 3

Mari: **Is it better than that?**
Uncle: **M ... maybe.**
Mari: **Is it a sad story?**
Uncle: **Terribly sad, but it's romantic and thrilling.**
Mari: **I didn't know there was a story like that.**
Uncle: **There is. Do you want to read it?**
Mari: **Absolutely. Where is it?**

terribly sad「とても悲しい」terrible は「ひどい」という形容詞だが、terribly と副詞になると悪い意味はなくなる。

I am terribly sorry to hear that.
It's terribly important for you to keep it.
「それを保存しておくことがとても大事です。」
They were terribly pleased to see their grandson.
「孫の顔が見れてとても喜んだ。」

a story like that「そのような話」

I don't know a singer like that.
I did't know there was a restaurant like that.
I didn't know you had a watch like that.

Do you want to read it?「読みたいと思いますか。」ごく平易な言い方のようだが、日本人は最後の it を落とし易いから注意。

Absolutely.「絶対、ぜひ」完全に同意見だという気持ちを表す慣用語。否定のときは not を付けて Absolutely not. と言う。

She is lovely, isn't she? — Absolutely.
What a beautiful baby! — Absolutely.
You haven't changed your mind, I hope? — Absolutely not.
「決心は変えていないのだろうね。」「変えるものか。」

Point 4

Uncle: **Well, it may come out in a month or so.**
Mari: **Then it's a new story. Who is it by?**
Uncle: **By Akio Aoki.**
Mari: **By you?**
Uncle: **Yes, I have entered a contest for the best novel.**
Mari: **And you won?**
Uncle: **I hope so. That's what I'm waiting for.**

come out「出る」これは be published と同じ意味。

in a month or so「一ヵ月かそこいらのうちに」
His book will come out in about half a year.
I'll be visiting you in a week or so.

Who is it by?「誰の作ですか。」本の著者でも、作曲家でも、作者をたずねるときは、Who is it by? でよい。文法的には who は whom となるべきだが、普通には who の方をよく使う。
Who did you see there? / Who did you play with?

I have entered a contest for ...「…の懸賞に応募している」まだ結果が発表になっていないから、現在完了形で言ったもの。発表後なら過去形で言う。
I have entered a contest for the best mystery.
We entered a chorus contest and won the second prize.

I hope so.「そうだといいが。」これも決まり文句。
Did you pass the exam in English? — I hope so.
Did she catch the plane? — I hope so.

That's what I'm waiting for.「それを私は待っている。」
That's what I think.「私もそう思います。」
That's what I said.「私は確かにそう言いました。」
That's exactly what I did.

実力チェック　　**英語で言ってみよう！**

1.「風と共に去りぬ」という映画を知っていますか。

2. マリリン・モンロー (Marilyn Monroe) という女優を知っていますか。

3. まあ、きれいな絵だこと。

4. あなたの猫はどうしたのですか。

5. そんな絵描きがいるとは知らなかった。

6. まさか君はそれを買ったと言うんじゃないだろうね。

平川唯一　英語の歌

Come, Come, Everybody

平川唯一作詞
中山晋平作曲
飯田信夫編曲

Come, come, everybody.
How do you do, and how are you?
Won't you have some candy,
One and two and three, four, five?
Let's all sing a happy song,
Sing tra la la la la.

Good-bye, everybody,
Good night until tomorrow.
Monday, Tuesday, Wednesday, Thursday,
Friday, Saturday, Sunday.
Let's all come and meet again,
Singing tra la la.

証城寺のたぬきばやし

野口雨情作詞（1924）
中山晋平作曲

証（しょう）、証（しょう）、証城寺（しょうじょうじ）
証城寺の庭は
ツ、ツ、月夜だ
みんな出て来い来い来い
おいらの友達ア
ぽんぽこぽんのぽん

負けるな、負けるな
和尚（おしょう）さんに負けるな
来い、来い、来い、来い来い来い
みんな出て、来い来い来い

証、証、証城寺
証城寺の萩（はぎ）は
ツ、ツ、月夜に花盛（はなざか）り
おいらは浮（う）かれて
ぽんぽこぽんのぽん

あとがき

1946 年から 5 年間、平川唯一氏が戦後の日本を明るくしようと思って放送されたカムカム英語は、家族の会話を題材にした、実に楽しく、役に立つ番組であった。当時平川先生の名は、日本中で総理大臣やマッカーサー司令官、美空ひばりと同じぐらい有名だった。実際、先生のご自宅にはファンレターが 50 万通も保管されていたという。

この平川先生の「カムカムエヴリバディ」との出会いが、その後の私の英文学者、英語教育者としての人生を切り開いてくれた。当時熊本の人吉高校二年生だった私は、自分の勉強に役立っているカムカム英語をぜひ下級生にも勉強してもらいたいとの思いから、校内に語学部を作った。当時の木造校舎（こうしゃ）の二階から狭（せま）い階段で上がっていく、物見櫓（ものみやぐら）のような部屋を部室として使わせてもらい、毎日昼休みに 20 名ほどが集まった。前日放送された内容を、平川先生の代わりに私が声に出し、みんなが声を揃（そろ）えて繰り返す。月曜日には前の週の放送を題材に、会話の言葉を私が日本語で言い、みんなが英語で答えるという試験もしていた。ただ放送をきくだけではなく、習った文章の一部を別の単語に替えて自由に使いこなせるようになってはじめて身に着いたと言えると考えたからである。

後年、熊本大学の教師になってから、県下の中学高校英語教員の再教育などに取り組んだ私は、1981 年以来、平川英語の復活にかかわり、本書も 1997 年に初版を出版している。また本書のストーリーを大学の通訳演習の教材として使い、これが立派な教材として大人にも役立つことを再確認することとなった。

平川英語の復活に取り組んでから40年目の今日再び、いつの時代にも通(つう)じるコミュニケーション英語教材として平川英語を世に送り出すことで、平川先生にいくばくかの恩返しができたのではないかと思っている。

1997年の本書の初出版の際より、平川家長男ヴィクター氏、次男の洌氏（NHK出版『カムカムエヴリバディ 平川唯一と「ラジオ英語会話」の時代』の著者でウクレレの名手）にはいろいろ相談にのっていただいた。今回再びカムカムエブリバディが脚光を浴びるタイミングで再出版されるにあたって、平川洌氏や南雲堂編集部の加藤敦氏には多大なご尽力をいただき、より楽しく使いやすい学習教材となった。寄稿していただいた各界の方々も含め、厚く御礼を申し上げる。

＊本書は、南雲堂より1997年に刊行された「平川唯一のファミリー イングリッシュ」に加筆・修正を加えたものです。

英語で言ってみよう［解答例］

Dialog 1: All Even

1. I'm in a hurry now.
2. That's why you are sweating.
3. You mean, you forgot your gloves at the store?
4. We all make mistakes now and then, don't we?
5. The Japanese people have worked hard to catch up with the big powers of the world.

Dialog 2: A Goat

1. It's a lot of trouble to feed birds.
2. I've had enough oranges already.
3. I'll speak to your teacher about it.
4. Why do you want a computer so much?
5. The prime minister said he would do his best.

Dialog 3: I Like Everything

1. For one thing, I like the weather here.
2. Shall we have *udon*?
3. What do you mean?
4. Say what you want like a man.
5. Japanese fifty years ago is a little different from what it is today.

Dialog 4: The Study of Sleep

1. Wait a minute. I'm drinking tea now.
2. I have to have some money before I can go.
3. That's because you're thirsty.
4. I never thought about that.
5. Life is like pushing a heavy wagon.

Dialog 5: Father's Birthday

1. I had almost forgotten it myself.
2. How did you remember?
3. Oh, that's how you contacted him?
4. There is one thing we've been planning for some time.
5. We are getting short on rice.

Dialog 6: A Giant Home Run

1. Here you are.
2. I walked all the way from the station.
3. I want a glass of beer on a hot day like this.
4. I'm not surprised. You see, he is rich.
5. You should have gone to the Madonna concert.

Dialog 7: A New Raincoat

1. Oh, that explains everything.
2. There's nothing strange in that.
3. How kind your father is!
4. He didn't seem to know you at all.
5. He must have been calling her for a long time.

Dialog 8: The Nobel Prize

1. Read what it says in this book.
2. No wonder you look sleepy.
3. I sleep late in the morning.
4. I have the habit of studying while listening to FM.
5. You have a pretty good chance of becoming a fine businessman.

Dialog 9: A Living Doll

1. I thought the typhoon was still in Okinawa.
2. What do you mean, "she"?

3. How do you know the package hasn't come yet?
4. I want you all to grow up just like that player.
5. Are you kidding me again?

Dialog 10: A Great Pitcher in the Making

1. Is this yours?
2. I can hardly wait.
3. I'll watch the baby while you work in the kitchen.
4. Dad is a very fast walker.
5. Let's see if we can use this personal computer.

Dialog 11: Father's Headache

1. Are you finished? — Oh, no. I have a long way to go yet.
2. Why don't you take a rest for a while?
3. There's something I have to do the day after tomorrow.
4. I need a whole day to copy it.
5. They would all be happier if I didn't go.

Dialog 12: When We Grow Up

1. We must first get up at seven o'clock.
2. That's why I am playing tennis every day.
3. What will you do if the electricity fails?
4. All you have to do is to speak to your teacher right away.
5. Who will volunteer to clean the rooms?

Dialog 13: Price for Every Home Run

1. Do you mean you've saved up one million yen?
2. I have enough money to pay expenses here.
3. I don't see how he can cook so well.
4. That restaurant is crowded every time I go.
5. You are sure to get into trouble if you drink too much.

Dialog 14: Seeing Hollywood in Three Minutes

1. The street was beautiful! Lined on both sides with pine trees.
2. That's the place where local goods are displayed.
3. That's where they make *sake*.
4. I wonder when they will come to Japan.
5. You may have a chance to see her sing Tosca.

Dialog 15: Looking for a Job

1. I see you broke this.
2. What sort of work are you doing now?
3. I don't see why not.
4. In that case I'll look for another job.
5. Anytime you say will be all right with me.
6. I reported to Professor Brown's office at 9:00 on Friday.

Dialog 16: Enjoying the Evening Cool

1. How was the concert?
2. I'll hang it up here.
3. What do you call this?
4. I've got a weekly magazine for you.
5. It was so lovely I almost bought it.

Dialog 17: A Bicycle Ride

1. Oh, it's you! I didn't know it was you.
2. There's nothing like this.
3. Why are you late again?
4. Japan had a hard time catching up with the world economy.
5. I guess you are right at that.
6. She has finally made it as an opera singer.

Dialog 18: A Good Skier

1. How are you coming on with your paper?
2. It'll all be finished in about two weeks.
3. Can you come to my house by four?
4. Where did you go in such a hurry?
5. I didn't know he was so wealthy.
6. I've never seen him study.

Dialog 19: Really Similar but Different

1. Mom said she would go shopping in the morning.
2. I can tell Dad by the way he walks.
3. Taro always does that.
4. For that matter, Jiro has the same habit, too.
5. That's because they are really similar.

Dialog 20: Waiting for Spring

1. Do you know the movie called "Gone with the Wind"?
2. Do you know the movie star called Marilyn Monroe?
3. Oh, what a beautiful painting!
4. What's the matter with your cat?
5. I didn't know there was a painter like that.
6. You don't mean you bought it, do you?

ラジオテキスト初出一覧

放送時期（昭和）

1　All Even　38号4週24年9月
2　A Goat　31号3週24年2月
3　I Like Everything　47号3週25年6月
4　The Study of Sleep　44号2週25年3月
5　Father's Birthday　10号4週22年10月
6　A Giant Home Run　1号3週21年2月
7　A New Raincoat　22号1週23年4月
8　The Nobel Prize　43号1週25年1月
9　A Living Doll　32号1週24年3月
10　A Great Pitcher in the Making　33号2週24年4月
11　Father's Headache　33号4週24年4月
12　When We Grow Up　21号2週23年3月
13　Price for Every Home Run　40号1週24年10月
14　Seeing Hollywood in Three Minutes　20号4週23年3月
15　Looking for a Job　18号3週23年1月
16　Enjoying the Evening Cool　7号4週21年8月
17　A Bicycle Ride　24号4週23年4月
18　A Good Skier　42号2週25年1月
19　Really Similar but Different　38号1週24年8月
20　Waiting for Spring　32号4週24年3月

（注）全54冊のラジオテキストは下記の本に復刻されている。
平川唯一著『カムカム英語　NHKラジオテキスト英語会話復刻版』名著普及会(1986年刊)、別冊解説福田昇八

活用語句索引

[数字は Dialog-Point 番号]

編者紹介

福田昇八（ふくだ・しょうはち）

1933年熊本県生まれ。東京大学英文科卒。熊本大学名誉教授。2012年、瑞宝中授章を受賞。2017年『韻文訳　妖精の女王』（九州大学出版会）で日本翻訳文化賞を受賞。主な著書に、『ビートルズの心』（共著、大修館書店）、『語学開国』（大修館書店）、『イギリス・アメリカ文学史』（南雲堂）、『英詩のこころ』（岩波書店）などがある。

平川洌（ひらかわ・きよし）

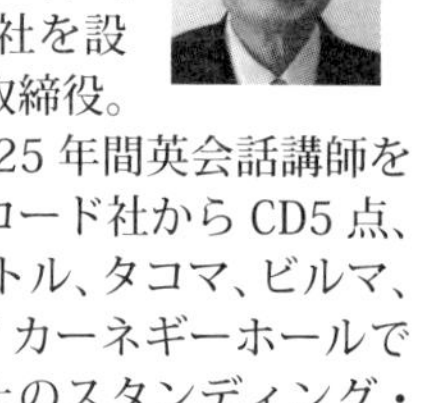

昭和16年、平川唯一の次男として東京・世田谷に生まれる。
昭和39年、自由学園最高学部経済学科卒業。同年、ホリー株式会社入社、貿易部に勤務。昭和50年、ホリー商事株式会社を設立し、全世界を相手にビジネス取引を展開。現在、同社代表取締役。カムカム英語センター・リーダー。慶應義塾外国語学校で25年間英会話講師を務めた。また、ウクレレの第一人者でもある。クラウンレコード社からCD5点、教則本3冊を出し、ドレミ出版より全国販売。ハワイ、シアトル、タコマ、ビルマ、オーストラリア、韓国等々、国内外で演奏活動をする。NYカーネギーホールでは日本人で初めてウクレレソリストとして出演、10分以上のスタンディング・オベイションを浴びる。現在、18の教室でウクレレ・ソロを教えている。持ち前の英語を使って正しいアメリカ英語の発音で英語の唄がうたえるように生徒を指導している。

校閲者紹介

Thomas Reid（トム・リード）

1950年コロラド州生まれ。プリンストン大学古典語科卒。1973-4年熊本県英語教育振興会講師、1990-95年ワシントン・ポスト極東総局長、後にロンドン総局長を歴任。著書に、『チップに組み込め』（草思社）、『誰も知らないアメリカ議会』（東洋経済新報社）、『トムの目　トムの耳』（講談社）などがある。

平川唯一（ひらかわただいち）のファミリーイングリッシュ
カムカムエヴリバディ

2021年10月14日　1刷

編者　福田昇八
平川洌
校閲　トム・リード

装丁・本文デザイン　銀月堂
表紙イラスト　ヨシオカ ユリ
編集　加藤敦

発行者　南雲一範
発行所　株式会社 南雲堂
〒 162-0801
東京都新宿区山吹町 361
TEL 03-3268-2384
FAX 03-3260-5425
印刷所　日本ハイコム株式会社
製本所　松村製本所

2021 Printed in Japan
ISBN978-4-523-26604-4　C0082　<1-604>

Email　nanundo@post.email.ne.jp
URL　https://www.nanun-do.co.jp

プロジェクトで学ぶ実践ビジネス英語

フルカラー!!
無料音声付き

寺内　はじめ編著

A5判　208ページ　定価1980円（本体1800円）

会社を救え、太郎君！

日本とアメリカのビジネス舞台で大活躍。

人工太陽光線開発プロジェクトスタート！

プロジェクトの企画・立案、
プレゼンテーション、クレーム対応までの
あらゆるシーンを網羅。
シミュレーションしながら鍛える
実践型ビジネス英語の決定版！

南雲堂
NAN'UN-DO